DISCOURSE SKILLS IN ENGLISH

for specialized purposes

Sookhe Kim

Daegu University Press

Sookhe Kim
Professor, Dept of English Education, Daegu University
University of California, Santa Barbara, USA, B.A.
University of California, Santa Cruz, USA, M.A.
Keimyoung University, Korea, Ph.D.

초　판 | 2009년 2월 20일
지은이 | 김숙희
펴낸이 | 이용두
펴낸곳 | 대구대학교출판부
경북 경산시 진량읍 내리리 15 대구대학교출판부
전화 053) 850-8661~4 | 팩스 053) 850-5669
홈페이지 주소 | http://dubookstore.daegu.ac.kr/
찍은곳 | 남경기획
ISBN 978-89-7794-502-9-93740
값 10,000원

Preface

The aim of this book is to provide students with a continuous flow of input that challenges their current knowledge of English language, thereby allowing them to progress naturally to a higher level of communicative competence. Throughout the process, the opportunities to discuss literary elements--such as theme, plot, characters, setting, tone, and point of view that are thoroughly expressed--will enable students to communicate their own thoughts, feelings and opinions that will derive from reading the essays.

Thus, these interactive discussions will naturally motivate students to use various communicational expressions as they exchange personal information that relate to the topics that are discussed in class. Without doubt, this learning approach, which significantly emphasizes communication, will help students to build confidence and fluency in an English-speaking environment.

Particular gratitude goes to Wesley and Janice Oh who have encouraged and helped complete the project. I also thank Daegu University Press for consistently encouraging me to achieve a successful manuscript.

ContentS

I

PERSONAL BACKGROUND

A | The Old Chinese Proverb

I'll always remember that one day after school when I had forgotten to do my homework again, prompting my teacher to talk to my dad. On looking back, I'm certain that dad recognized the obduracy from my glaring eyes. His stern expression softened up unexpectedly, and he stated a Chinese proverb, which roughly translates to: "If when young one doesn't work hard, when older one will regretfully rub his aching back." Then he just walked towards the car, and I obediently followed, lost in thought.

Ever since I was young, dad has been instilling in me a thirst for challenge. He'd always give me math problems and leave novels on my bed. If I ever felt resentful of these tasks, he'd just repeat that Chinese proverb. Whenever he did that, fear would grab me, and I'd get to work.

Perhaps that's why I've always liked tackling challenges, and that's why in high school I have taken advantage of all opportunities available to extend myself. Not satisfied with the course selection at school, I participated in distance learning programs and went to different colleges, taking nine extra classes, including three extra AP classes. My search for challenge extends beyond academics. In middle school I was known as the kid in a corner in the library everyday playing Magic cards during lunch. Although that's still a hobby of mine, in high school I challenged myself to break out of my shell. I transformed myself from an introverted geek into the host of student events at my school, leading the crowd's cheers and riding on their wave of excitement.

Dad has stopped saying that proverb now, and I think that's because I've finally learned my lesson. I don't want to regret anything later on. So with every opportunity, I test myself beyond constraints. I'm not sure where I will end up later in life, but I think as of right now it doesn't matter, as long as I keep challenging myself. Hopefully I'll be a successful individual who isn't regretfully rubbing his back thinking about what could have been.

Reading and Discussion

*** Answer the following questions based on the passage.**

1. Can you think of any Chinese proverbs that are often mentioned by your parents?

2. What is your favorite proverb now days? Why did you choose that as your favorite?

3. Do you have a motto/guiding principle in your life.

4. Who is your motivating force in your life?

Exercise A:

* **Make sentences about yourself using the following expressions.**

a. tackling challenges:

b. taking advantages of all opportunities:

c. to break out of my shell:

d. a thirst for challenge:

e. test myself beyond constraints:

Exercise B:

*** Define the following words in English.**

a. proverb

b. obduracy

c. obediently

d. introverted

Exercise C:

*** Write a short summary of the passage**

B The Genuine Meaning of Grades

Shoulders hunched over, hood over head, I slowly trudged home. Every once in a while, I stopped and let out a sigh. Silently, I wondered, how could I have messed up so badly? As my body went into autopilot in the comfortable familiarity of my route home, my mind painfully raced back to the unsettling turn of events.

Although aware of the challenges in high school, as a sophomore, I felt like I was in complete control of my schoolwork. Some classes were known to be relatively easy, in particular the required World Literature class. After a few weeks, I had come to the same conclusion, so I promptly allocated my time elsewhere. I ended up adding two distance learning AP courses from the Center for Talented Youth: AP Chemistry and AP Physics. As the semester dragged on, my numerous activities took their toll on me, but the maintenance of straight A's for the majority of the semester made me feel that I was in total control of my busy schedule.

That was such a false hope. My stainless academic was not as stable as my overconfidence suggested. Because of the minimal amount of time I was putting into World Literature so I could concentrate on my other work, my grade was borderline. However, I kept telling myself everything was under control because I had received stellar scores on all my essays. I appeased myself with the thought that I would be able to work out everything in the end. Again, I did a mediocre job on the course's take-home final, opting to spend more time on other finals. To my utter dismay, I found out the week after that my less than satisfactory work had dipped my grade to an 89.6%, my first B in any class. Shaking from the shock, I approached the teacher after class, asking her to re-evaluate my final, or to possibly work out some deal based on my participation and activeness in class. It was then that she showed me my abysmal record in her class. All the small assignments and quizzes that I had half-heartedly worked through due to time constraints had added up over the course of the semester, resulting in a noticeable loss of points. Because of my active participation in class, she had also come to the conclusion that I had not been working as hard as I should have. She refused all of my entreaties. With tears stinging in my eyes, I listlessly limped out of her classroom. I felt like nothing was going right, and that it was all over for me.

I went back to her classroom for days, but each time my teacher became more adamant in her refusal. After a tumultuous period of bouts of anger, cries of injustice, and rounds of self-pity, something just clicked in my mind. With the help of my teacher and parents, I looked inwards and found the reasons of my failure rooted inside myself. It was a culmination of overconfidence, complacency, and lack of strong commitment throughout the semester. Moreover, I was able to come to terms with the fact that I would not get away with overstretching myself in my numerous activities. I dropped the AP Physics outside of school, and set out to re-prioritize my schedule. From that time on, I vowed to give everything the time and respect it deserved.

Once upon a time, I thought I was invincible. I had the misconceived notion that I would succeed in everything I do. Naively, I thought I could maintain my straight-A record easily. I realize now that I should never skirt the edge of danger like I did that semester, especially if I can avoid doing so with proper planning. I am human, which means I can't expect to be perfect, but I can work towards perfection if I retain humility.

At the time, I felt that the world was crumbling down on me. Since then, I have also learned to compose myself. It's okay if I can't have a perfect record. I just need to always prepare for my next challenge. Dawdling on prior mistakes is only a waste of time and emotions.

On looking back I am grateful to my first B experience. I learned and matured on that experience. Life will always have successes and failures, not only in the past, but also in the future. Now I have a better attitude in the face of future challenges, positive and negative.

Although I am slightly disappointed that I can't boast a straight–A record, that first B actually shines in my mind now as a positive and necessary step in my growth.

Reading and Discussion

*** Answer the following questions based on the passage.**

1. Have you ever experienced something similar to the passage above?

2. Are the grades you have received from the college are really important to you? How important are they?

3. Have you ever felt in your life that you have received a grade unfairly?

4. Do you have any regrets over your grades?

5. What do you regret the most in your life?

6. What lessons have you gotten from your careless mistakes?

Exercise A:

* **Make sentences about yourself using the following expressions.**

a. let out a sigh:

b. took their toll on me:

c. in total control of my busy schedule:

d. listlessly limped out of her class:

e. re-prioritize my schedule:

f. went into autopilot:

g. had a misconceived notion:

h. skirt the edge of danger:

Exercise B:

*** Define the following words in English.**

a. false hope

b. stellar

c. mediocre

d. abysmal record

e. tumultuous

Exercise C:

*** Write a short summary of the passage.**

C The Dark Tunnel

I was trapped in a dark tunnel, odious and endless.

Tears alone could not express my frustration. Neither could my shrieks and piercing cries loosen the tight ball of stress lodged in my stomach. I remember writhing on the kitchen floor every single day, throwing tantrums until I fell asleep from exhaustion and misery. My life had sunk to its nadir and my immaturity denied me the tools for my revival.

I desperately cried for help but I could not be heard. No help was on its way, so I was to escape on my own.

After spending 9 years of my life in Korea, I was shipped back to my birthplace, the US, on a plane for a "vacation". As the airport doors slid open in California, I took a deep breath of air. The smell was alien, like air-freshener and damp forest floors. The sun's rays on my skin were loaded with a perfection of warmth and comfort, the same kind of warmth and comfort the people around me draped me with. They treated me with courtesy and gleamed at me with ivory white smiles. The sounds that came from American mouths were gibberish to me but their gestures reassured me that I was in a safe and welcoming place.

I could not tell where people were from or what language they spoke but through the confusion I came to appreciate the term "American". Multi-culturalism was evident in the mixed skin tones that made up large crowds and in the variety of tastes in the restaurants. The food was sweet and flavourful, contrary to spicy Korean food. Many things I saw again for the first time. Fruits and vegetables had a new freshness and their colors were brighter. Sour green grapes were an exotic and strange fruit. People lived in houses rather than apartments. Their daily habits were peculiarities to me, their mundane chores were objects of curiosity. Most drove their Mercedes and Honda Civics for the shortest trips rather than walking or cycling. I was living in an unfamiliar world, both thrilled and anxious about my dislocation and my estrangement from my parents.

I had been left at a cave's mouth that led to a dark passageway. Feeling restless and attracted by the chance of adventure I was enticed by the cave's fug and hollow, pregnant silence. I followed the pathway with only my intuition as compass, disregarding the absence of my parents' protection.

Then I entered grade school. Making friends was a challenge as my English extended no further than general greetings. Schoolwork took hours of struggle: writing ten sentences about my weekend took me an hour and I spent half an hour to complete 15 pages of Dr Seuss. So I was bound to the house, doing homework and listening to vocabulary tapes. During class discussions I ran simple sentences through my head incessantly to guard against grammatical pitfalls. Yet my insecurity still prevented me from speaking, rendering me a silent observer. My face glowed cherry red whenever my grammar or pronunciation was corrected. Then at home I would explode in tears of frustration and shame. The everyday challenges that I had keenly anticipated just a few months earlier were now objects of dread.

Thinking that I had walked too deep into the tunnel, I turned. Where there had been light there was now only dark. I retrod my route over and over in my head but mistrusted my judgment. Grunting and whimpering, I tried to feel my way back to the light at the cave's mouth. But my fingertips were dumb to my senses, my memory and sight muddled by panic and distress.

To revive me from despair and fatigue, my parents constantly reassured me through the phone that I was a strong girl. They had faith that I could fight and overcome hardship. But entering middle school with elementary school English I was doomed. The ante was then raised further. I was accepted into the Gifted and Talented Program at Hyde Middle School. The subjects were varied and the competition fierce. Silicon Valley's academic elite were a diverse collection. Their fluency intimidated me and envy at their knowledge of American history festered within me. I studied harder than ever before, memorizing huge stores of vocabulary and leaving behind me a trail of work books, "English : The Easy Way". The burden of my labours grew weightier. Novels and short story collections made piles on my desk, in the bathroom and in the car. I spoke persistently and endlessly with anybody who let me, be they relaxing in the park, eating in McDonalds or at their grocery shopping.

I had to get out. Prostrating myself, crying and agonizing were fruitless. I raised my self up. My weak knees gave beneath me but I restored myself, returned to my full height and groped my way to a barricade of rocks and started to heave them behind me. My body and senses sought light and whispered prayers pushed me on. Dear God, help me prevail.

I grew with the years. Getting stronger and smarter, I surpassed my peers in life fulfillment and study. English was now my enabler. School work was no longer the bane of my days. Thus, I push myself to reach out further than just academics. In the wake of my blossoming, I nurtured a need to shape student life for those around me. I took several leadership positions in class councils and in the

Santa Clara Youth Task Force, promoting school spirits and youth rights along the way. My life was touched by the tragedy of cancer, provoking me to respond; I am now the president of the Tino Cancer Society. Basketball relieved stress and I earned my way to the captaincy and MVP of my team. Responsibility and endurance have marked my efforts in all I do and my struggles with English have shaped and strengthened my character. I now stand tall, an independent and driven individual who cherishes cultural diversity and appreciates the benefits that can grow from the adversities of life. I am ready to encounter tougher challenges and achieve greater goals.

The last rock was set aside and I emerged, my eyes blinking in the daylight. The bright world that I had momentarily departed now lay before me. I had reawakened. My sense of achievement tempered by lingering wariness, I looked out over a field of trees. Shame grew within me: I had neglected nature's gifts. Perhaps God had contrived my trials. Alongside my shame then grew a new vista of, and lust for, life. My burden lifted, my steps were lightened. Cautiously I stepped forward then gained speed with my new-found strength. Arms thrown wide I ran down to the field and through the trees.

Reading and Discussion

*** Answer the following questions based on the passage.**

1. Do you know what analogy is? Do you enjoy reading the writing styles such as this?

2. What does the dark tunnel symbolize?

3. What feelings do you get from reading the passage?

4. Have you ever felt so depressed in your life? Describe why you were feeling depressed.

5. What was the turning point in your life? What was so special about that experience?

6. Explain the given sentence: "The burden of my labours grew weightier." What are your burdens in your life?

Exercise A:

* **Make sentences about yourself using the following expressions.**

a. throwing tantrums:

b. my immaturity denied me:

c. objects of curiosity:

d. guard against grammatical pitfalls:

e. had keenly anticipated:

f. objects of dread:

g. I was doomed:

h. nurtured a need to shape student life:

i. cherishes cultural diversity

Exercise B:

*** Define the following words in English.**

a. Multi- culturalism:

b. mundane chores:

c. fierce:

d. prostrating:

e. adversity

f. diversity

Exercise C:

*** Write a short summary of the passage.**

D The Rafting

Go all the way down to the end of Stevens Creek and turn onto Foothill Boulevard. Hope to survive a few blind turns and loops in the hills on a narrow one lane road, and the reservoir will appear on the left side. Then unload the raft from the mess of knots that will hopefully have kept it secure on top of the car and glide it into the cool blue water. Navigate, or at least attempt to navigate, around three bends. A nice tall tree that hangs over the water will come into view. Climb up the nailed-in wooden planks on the tree trunk, and grab the rope. Take a deep breath, ready your loudest Tarzan roar, and take a leap of faith…

"Hey you guys, let's go rafting". That was not quite what I expected Max to say when we were at his house after a scrumptious barbeque dinner. I wasn't quick to respond to his random suggestion. However, Max insisted, and when I thought about it, rafting for a couple hours would definitely be more fun than lounging around in his house complaining about having nothing to do. After loading up all our gear, we headed up to the nearby reservoir.

The four of us guys got into the raft and started rowing hurriedly towards Max's "surprise" location. Then, the rope swing came into view. It felt like we were living back in the time of Tom Sawyer and that we had the chance to live one of his adventures for ourselves. Immediately, we stripped down and excitedly clambered up the shore and onto the tree planks.

"Actually you guys, it looks a lot scarier when you climb up, someone else come do it."

"Jeez man, don't be lame… but I don't want to go first either. Hey, make James go."

Rarely do boys consider everyone's opinion when making group decisions, so naturally I had no say now. Nervously, I climbed up the shaky planks that were nailed into the tree, and grabbed the knotted rope.

"Here, James, I'll count for you. Ready? On three. One, two…"

Time to take the leap of faith. It's now or never. Opportunities come and go, and you've got to be able to take a risk when you get the chance. You can't let down your friends, can you? More importantly, you can't let yourself down. Don't ever back down from a challenge. I could have backed down instead of running against the incumbent class president at the time. It wasn't necessary for me to run against him, but I wanted to improve our class council and challenging him would get me there. *If you don't try, you won't suffer any repercussions, but think about the benefits if you do take the chance.* Sometimes you've just got to take a risk. *Go for it James, go.*

"…Three!"

I jumped off of the tree, gripping onto the rope with all my strength. Once I felt like I had reached the top of my upward pendulum-like swing, I unleashed my greatest Tarzan roar and let go of the rope, splashing into the clear blue water below me. The icy coldness enveloped me, and a searing pain flashed through my chest.

Watch out for the negative consequences. Maybe jumping off of that rope wasn't the best idea after all. I was reminded of the resentment and doubt I received when I joined the school's competitive wrestling team in my sophomore year. I wanted to take advantage of wrestling as a physically and mentally demanding sport that could teach me valuable life lessons. The coaches and wrestlers all thought I was crazy for joining the sport so late, but I made it a point to change their attitudes as time went by. Although I turned out to be pretty mediocre at best, I am proud that I took the chance, because I really have learned more than just wrestling.

"Oh my god, he screamed out in pain!"

"James, how was it?"

I knew it would be worth it. As I resurfaced, the broadest grin of satisfaction stretched my face. As soon as the initial shock wore away, I could hear the voices of my friends yelling and cheering in the distance. It reminded me of the flattering ovation I received at Tino Stock, a student concert at school that I helped organize and participated in. During the performance, I had a saxophone solo, which I was considering skipping because the large crowd made me unsure of my abilities. When I heard the musical cue though, I knew that not playing the solo just wasn't an option, and I let my passion for my music overtake my fear as I belted out my own melody. It was scary diving in with so much passion and without any inhibitions, but this made me realize how gratifying taking that chance could be. I ran the risk of making myself a fool, but instead of mentioning the off-tune high notes, everybody came up to me and complimented the beauty of my solo. *Now share it with the world, James.*

"Dude, he's not responding. Really, how was it?"

With a devilish grin, I finally replied, "Oh I don't know, how about… excellent?"

Needless to say, the four of us entertained ourselves by swinging on the rope for quite a while. Every time the stakes got higher as we added louder shouts, twists, turns and flips. Finally, after dislocating a finger, turning red all over our bodies from bad landings in the water, and nearly drowning by getting caught in a plant, we decided that we had our fill and languidly paddled back as the sun was abandoning us. We left our Tom Sawyer rope swing, promising it that we'd come back another day. I don't know if the experience will still be the same if we ever do go back. Luckily, as I encounter my own different Tom Sawyer rope swing situations, that original experience will remain engrained in my mind and be a constant reminder to myself to just take the leap of faith, and splash into the icy unknown.

Reading and Discussion

*** Answer the following questions based on the passage.**

1. In your opinion, how well does the writer replaces himself with Tom Sawyer?

2. Have you ever taken any chances in your life? How risky was it?

3. What were the benefits of taking chances in your life?

4. Do you have a true friend who is willing to take chances with you?

5. Do you have any childhood experiences that are engrained in your memory?

6. Describe your hometown. Are there any creeks/reservoir near your hometown?

Exercise A:

* **Make sentences about yourself using the following expressions.**

a. take a leap of faith:

b. be lame:

c. suffer any repercussions:

d. icy coldness enveloped me:

e. searing pain flashed through my chest:

f. watch out for the negative consequences:

g. music overtakes my fear:

h. ran the risk:

i. sun abandoning us:

j. grained in my mind:

Exercise B:

*** Define the following words in English.**

a. scrumptious:

b. incumbent:

c. pendulum:

d. Tarzan roar:

e. musical cue:

f. devilish grin:

Exercise C:

* **Write a short summary of the passage.**

E The Second Generation

I am a Korean girl, yet my English speaking abilities far surpass my Korean. Both of my parents speak Korean. I adore Korean cuisine and watch Korean programs but wish to carry my future interests into the world of English and journalism. Being an American-born Asian does have its downfalls: my native language skills are lacking; I cannot fully communicate with my relatives; and I find myself dangling off into the branches of American society as my Korean roots lose grasp. As my father struggled to maintain a Korean influence within our home and my perfectionist mother demanded structure, I began to realize that I was completely different from both of my parents. As much as I accept the ideals my parents have taught me, I have discovered that journalism is the field where I can fully embrace my much-needed desire for freedom and exploration. Without the realization of what journalism allows me to fulfill, I would have never truly realized my aspirations for the future.

Since the moment I held my first article, staring at it in the school newspaper, I felt a rush of ecstasy and pure enjoyment. I was absolutely amazed at the power our paper held. The responses from families, teachers, and students were immediate and demonstrated genuine interest in our article choices. It was through their feedback that I learned how important it is for a writer to present an accurate and sincere article to his or her readers. On one occasion, our staff printed an article that apparently offended student council members as it wrongly quoted a student thereby implying that the council was corrupt and unnecessary. The situation led to heated arguments and complaints, causing a mess of frustration and misunderstanding. This experience opened my eyes to the vital necessity of clarity between the writer and reader. It allowed me to realize why clear communication is important and also what it can create: When a newspaper becomes a reliable and trustworthy source, readers will look towards it for guidance and actually want to read the opinions and perspectives on current events. I want to develop and pursue this author–audience relationship and express my ideas through this communication.

Journalism has placed me in a state of both perplexity and awe– It is as if an entire new world has been revealed to me; through journalism that I have learned I am neither limited to five paragraph essays nor forbidden to use personal pronouns; I have been given the opportunity and freedom to write what I please. I utterly love and embrace, with every article I coin, the independence and liberty journalism, and writing in general, allows me to use.

As an editor this year, I am learning more about the field and polishing my writing abilities as well. I am also constantly discovering more about myself. Just as I have learned how much I differ from my parents, I have also realized who I truly am: A whimsical–unformatted–Korean–American who wishes to explore the nooks and crannies of writing and seek diverse expressions and perspectives on it. I respect and love my parents very much, but I ache to take chances unlike my mother and not to limit myself to a single culture like my father. I am in no way proclaiming myself to be an exemplary writer– I simply want to share my opinions, my writing style, my perceptions, and my thoughts with others through my literary works. I hope to continue this path of self–discovery as I cultivate my journalistic passion in my future academics.

Reading and Discussion

*** Answer the following questions based on the passage.**

1. According to the passage, how does the second generation views the world differently from the first generation?

2. Do you know what journalism is?

3. How does sociological concept of Melting Pot different from Salad Bowl? In your opinion, which concept applies better in his/her situation?

4. Have you ever written any articles to be published?

5. If you have a chance to write a newspaper to be published, what topics would you consider writing about? Why?

Exercise A:

* **Make sentences about yourself using the following expressions.**

a. have its downfall:

b. dangling off into the branches of American society:

c. felt a rush of ecstasy and pure enjoyment:

d. utterly love and embrace:

e. explore the nooks and crannies of writing:

f. ache to take chances:

Exercise B:

* **Define the following words in English.**

a. journalism:

b. aspirations:

c. corrupt:

d. trustworthy source:

e. perplexity and awe:

f. whimsical−unformatted−Korean−American:

Exercise C:

*** Write a short summary of the passage.**

박성린 작

F A Personal Pleasure

One predilection I have since I was little is the penchant for reading. I regularly read fiction, non–fiction, and periodicals such as *Time*, *Newsweek*, and *Fortune*. This compulsion started perhaps when my parents teased my curiosity by constant stories of the *Arabian Nights*, Hans Christian Andersen and Grimm Brothers. Or it started perhaps with my elementary school teacher Mr. Redman's love for Edgar Allen Poe. However it got started, the higher grades I go, the more avid a reader I have become. I began reading Homer, Dickens and Cervantes in sixth grade, Steinbeck, Hemingway and the Bronte sisters in the 7th, and Kafka, Camus and Dosdoyesvky by the 8th.

The summer before I entered high school, I began the voluntary Merit Reader Program sponsored by the high school. It required reading six classic novels and writing a review for each. I have consistently finished all requirements with excitement for every summer since then. By now, I have read eighty classic books in literature. Every reading is a new pleasure and a new experience in life. As an indiscriminate reader, I have honed my reading skills to be discerning, appreciating the myriad subtle life experiences poignant to each writer. To paraphrase Sir Francis Bacon, for me, reading serves for delight, for ornament, and for ability.

Reading and Discussion

*** Answer the following questions based on the passage.**

1. Are there any books you have read and still stay in your memory?

2. Are you presently reading any books/magazines? Do you wish to recommend them to your friends?

3. What genre of writings do you enjoy reading the most?

4. Have you read any books that are mentioned in the passage?

Exercise A:

*** Make sentences about yourself using the following expressions.**

a. teased my curiosity:

b. indiscriminate reader:

c. have honed my reading skills to discerning:

Exercise B:

*** Define the following words in English.**

a. predilection:

b. compulsion:

c. avid reader:

d. penchant:

e. myriad:

f. poignant

g. paraphrase:

Exercise C:

* Write a short summary of the passage.

G Significant Challenges

Ever since I was young, my father has been instilling a thirst for challenges. He'd always give me difficult math problems to work on, and leave classic novels on my bed for me to tackle. If I ever felt resentful of my father's pressure, he'd always say his favorite Chinese proverb, which roughly translates to, "If when young one doesn't work hard, when older one will regretfully rub his aching back." Whenever he said that, fear would immediately grab my heart, and I'd get working. He's stopped saying that phrase now, and I think that's because I've finally learned my lesson. I don't want to regret anything later on in life, so with every opportunity I get I try to test myself and go beyond what is necessary.

I like challenges. Freshman year I went to Community College to take Spanish and advance further in a harder high school course. I got a slap from reality the next year when I had to struggle in a much higher level Spanish course at my high school. I enjoyed the challenge though, not being entirely unprepared after my summer course, and achieved a relieving sense of accomplishment as I got through my first semester. The next summer I went to college to take Macro economics and Oral Spanish at a higher level, both of which seemed demanding. This past summer I took Linear Algebra and Vector Calculus because I had finished my school's math courses. My guidance counselor told me that it was unnecessary to take an even higher math course, but I felt the need to challenge myself. That math course would be challenging, and I felt like I needed that intellectual stimulation. Otherwise I would feel lazy, unproductive, and most of all, unfaithful to my pursuit of challenge.

My search for challenges extends beyond academics. In middle school, I was an extremely shy guy who didn't participate in outside activities. I questioned why I acted that way in high school, so I challenged myself to extend my personal boundaries. I set out to not just participate in sports and student events, but be a leader in all my endeavors. My first season as a wrestler ended in complete failure with only one win as the weak-link wrestler on our extremely competitive team. Despite my discouraging record and my peers telling me to look elsewhere for "personal improvement", I persisted, challenging myself to become a league champion the next year. I didn't succeed in my goal, but I trained hard enough that the coach recognized me and made me a captain of the junior varsity squad as well as giving me the Coach's Award for most improved.

It also became a challenge to myself to become proactive. Often, because I wasn't a familiar face, all my antics received little attention, and people ridiculed rather than respected me. After licking my wounds though, I'd come back determined that this was not going to be a challenge that I couldn't meet. My enthusiasm eventually garnered some support, and I quickly got involved with many activities and always tried to help out wherever I could. As I kept challenging myself to improve myself, my desire to help quickly grew into a desire to lead others to success. The next year I was elected Class President, and because of the recognition I got from the challenging goals I set for myself as Class President, I was elected ASB Vice President the next year. Promoting spirit and motivating students to have fun in activities has become my passion, and I keep challenging myself to make even greater contributions and making school more enjoyable for the student body.

It felt natural to join marching band when I entered high school because I enjoyed playing the Alto Saxophone. I was really just a mediocre member of the saxophone section at both playing and marching, so changing that became another goal of mine. I went to all the extra practices for band as well as religiously practicing at home. By the end of the season I was not only an excellent marcher, but had also risen to second chair.

Sophomore year I was chosen to be section leader. Later on, I took the initiative to start a student Band organization to help integrate the Marching Band into the student body, and was elected as Band President when I succeeded in founding the organization.

I'm not too sure of what my career path will end up being down the road, but as of right now it honestly doesn't matter, as long as I challenge myself. Hopefully I'll be a successful individual who loves a challenge and isn't regretfully rubbing his back thinking about better days.

Reading and Discussion

*** Answer the following questions based on the passage.**

1. Do you like challenges?

2. What are your personal/academic boundaries?

3. Have you done anything to expand your boundaries?

Exercise A:

* **Make sentences about yourself using the following expressions.**

a. instilling a thirst for challenges:

b. for me to tackle:

c. grab my heart:

d. a slap from reality:

e. extend my personal boundaries:

f. a leader in all my endeavors:

g. ridiculed rather than respected:

h. took the initiative to start:

Exercise B:

*** Define the following words in English.**

a. resentful:

b. intellectual stimulation:

c. pursuit of challenge:

d. proactive:

Exercise C:

*** Write a short summary of the passage.**

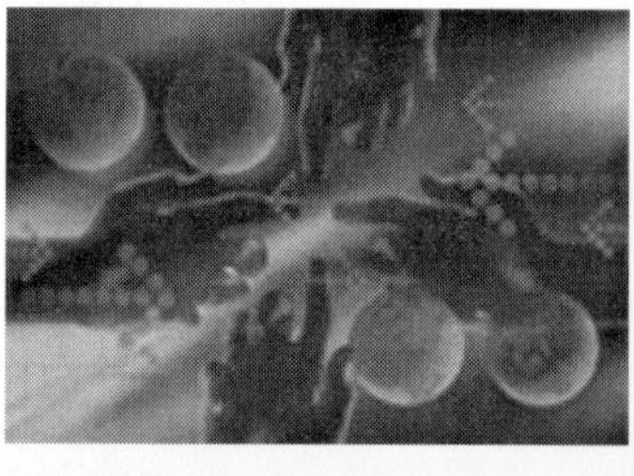

II
INFLUENTIAL PERSON

A | A Brother of Mine

He was my mentor and coach, brother and best friend.

We hung out in his room on weekends, listening to music and playing video games. He corrected my shooting form as he re-bounded my free-throws. His interests, speech, actions, and thoughts almost imperceptibly shaped my own. And every week, for two consecutive hours, he sat me down at a desk and guided me through algebra's labyrinths.

Wesley and I were complete opposites: I was the chubby, outgoing and witty kid, he the lanky, studious schoolboy, quiet and detached. He didn't say much, but his words were measured and worth listening to and I harbored a jealousy of his academic prowess. I see now that his was quite a juggling act, his one hand securing my safety net, the other raising the bar for my achievements.

As he entered his second year of high school, Wesley made choices that inadvertently affected my life. He strayed away from schoolwork, distracted by sports and music. His grades dropped. The consequent admonitions only made him downhearted and unapproachable. Criticism deflected off him as he became more withdrawn. The days of basketball and computer games were long over, our kinship abandoned.

The decline in his grades leveled off before edging back up. It was then I realized his academic expertise hadn't been effortless but hard-won. Sneaking peeks, I witnessed him devouring textbooks and posting never-ending vocabulary reminders on the walls. I admired his quiet discipline and perseverance.

In freshman year, I was lured from my true interests by standard High School diversions. I occupied myself with interests that weren't mine and struggled to be someone I wasn't. My grades plummeted. The new persona I wore didn't seem to fit. An anxious Wesley told me something that lodged in my mind: "You have to do better than what I did." His foray into sports and music at the expense of his longer term ambitions had left him unfulfilled. He had failed others' expectations of him and he warned me of the greater pain in failing to live up to our expectations of ourselves. Wesley believed in my abilities. He broke my fall and hauled me to my feet.

Just as his grades had improved, so did mine, Wesley again tugging and prodding me to higher goals. I had my best friend back! Certainly we both occupied ourselves with video games and basketball shootouts, late-night music video sessions and friends. But we had found balance.

Although he is away now, happy at college, he is still a constant presence. Wesley sparked the motivation in me by discreetly revealing his concern and my success in school is founded on what he taught me. That which truly interests and inspires us deserves our dedication and will be rewarded by that dedication. Tempting fads are disposable whereas discipline and determination bring a longer-lasting reward. Wesley shaped me in an ineffable way but the most precious thing he gave me is the clear vision I now possess.

Inferences

＊ Answer the following questions based on the passage.

1. Do you have any brothers or sisters in your family?

2. How are you different/similar to your siblings?

3. Have they made any significant influence over your life?

4. What changes have they brought into your life?

5. Do you have a mentor in your life?

6. Has anybody in your life "broke your fall and hauled you to your feet?"

Exercise A:

* **Make sentences about yourself using the following expressions.**

a. harbored a jealously of his academic prowess:

b. deflected off:

c. grades leveled off:

d. told me something that lodged in my mind:

e. tugging and prodding me to higher goals:

Exercise B:

∗ Define the following words in English.

a. imperceptibly:

b. juggling act:

c. inadvertently:

d. admonitions:

e. devouring:

f. perseverance:

g. plummeted:

Exercise C:

∗ Write a short summary of the passage.

B | Mrs. Merrick

Mrs. Merrick is a teacher at my school who lives a life of liveliness and spontaneity. Her class was my last class of the day last year, and rather than dragging my feet into the classroom and looking up at the whiteboard with swollen eyes because of the toll the long school day has had on me, my brain turns on and I feel like it's first period again. Mrs. Merrick is jumping up and down, gesticulating wildly about with her arms trying to describe to us the feelings of horror that Hester Prynne had when she encountered her husband. When she teaches, the students turn into munchkins and she becomes the Good Witch (as opposed to the Wicked Witch of the West that the average, dull, English teacher tends to be). The person I admire is the epitome of this exuberance, and celebrates each and every second of life. After all, what is life if we do not choose to live it? She was really the one that taught me how to love literature for not just the story, but also the language, the symbolism, and the meaning. It was with her that I really began to craft my essays with care and with a strong focus. She would always impose some thought–provoking topic to get the class intrigued and fired up in debate. Mrs. Merrick truly accomplishes what I think a teacher's main goal should be, to instill a passion and love for learning in all her students. I know for a fact that I am one of those students.

Inferences

*** Answer the following questions based on the passage.**

1. Who is your favorite teacher? What subject did he/she teach?

2. How did he/she become your favorite?

3. Is he/she still your idol?

4. What do you think a teacher's main goal should be?

5. Do you know Hester Prynne? Who is she?

Exercise A:

*** Make sentences about yourself using the following expressions.**

a. life of liveliness and spontaneity:

b. the epitome of this exuberance:

c. intrigued an fired up in debate:

d. instill a passion and love for learning:

Exercise B:

*** Define the following words in English.**

a. imperceptibly:

b. gesticulating wildly:

c. thought-provoking topic:

Exercise C:

* Write a short summary of the passage.

C An Old Friend

It's hard for me to admire someone in his or her entirety. I can always find something wrong with the "Golden Boy", or the famous world leader. If someone was to find a cure for cancer, I probably still would not admire him because of some other fault of his, like a lack of charisma. The disease of being far too critical probably stems from my gigantic ego and the unwillingness to concede defeat that comes from it. However there is one person that I do let my guard down with and I do give my utmost respect to, because everything about him is admirable.

Persistently working towards improving himself, the person I admire is a diligent man. Just like my father, this person has a passion for learning anything in an effort to broaden his horizons. My father has always told me that the key to success is in education. Even though he already has a job and a family, he still finds time to pursue his extra interests, like learning Spanish or reading up on Chinese history. The person I admire embraces the same ideals my father has about education, learning, and diligence. I try to emulate my idol by devoting myself to my schoolwork, be it in the subject areas of Biology, Spanish, or English literature.

A life filled with only learning is not enough, because one needs to go out and interact with others in the community. In this respect, the person I admire is much like David Joiner, a former student at my school who is two years older than me and has already graduated. David was a popular individual at my school, and he was involved in all sorts of extracurricular activities, like marching band and student government. He was a leader in all of the organizations he was involved in. This position of respect was not given to him haphazardly, but rather for his genuine kindness and sincerity when he dealt with people. He is a natural leader, and carried through on all his promises to lead those groups towards greatness. That same benevolence and leadership ability that David possess are key characteristics of the person I admire. As a leader and a follower, I know the importance of character and charisma, and anyone who has these traits are worthy of my reverence. The characteristics that truly make my hero shine amidst his work ethic and leadership are his energy and vivacity.

Inferences

*** Answer the following questions based on the passage.**

1. Who do you admire the most in your life?

2. What characteristics/attributes does that person possess?

3. Do agree with the expression: the key to success is in education?

4. Do you have a friend who has the similar characteristics that David possesses?

Exercise A:

*** Make sentences about yourself using the following expressions.**

a. stems from my gigantic ego:

b. unwillingness to concede defeat:

c. effort to broaden his horizons:

d. try to emulate my idol

Exercise B:

*** Define the following words in English.**

a. charisma:

b. diligent:

c. haphazardly:

d. benevolence:

e. reverence:

f. work ethic

g. vivacity

Exercise C:

* Write a short summary of the passage.

Ⅲ
SIGNIFICANT QUALITY

A. The Leadership

B. The Wrestling Match

C. The Golden Opportunity

D. The Tutoring Experience

E. The Band Competition

F. The Spirit Committee

A The Leadership

The one quality I have that most exercises my talent, displays my accomplishments and enables my contributions to society is that of leadership.

I have always maintained a good balance between my academic and social lives volunteering for community events and school activities. I boost my class' spirit and pride by organizing fundraisers, cheers and social events. I have been field conductor of the school band and choreographed the class of 2009 girls' homecoming dance as well as much else in between, being prominent on the basketball court both playing point guard and cheering for the Varsity boys.

My active life has continued beyond the school boundaries. At the request of a friend I joined the Tino Cancer Society. Back then, cancer was for me a distant menace: then my uncle, who helped raise me, was diagnosed with prostate cancer. The menace had intruded upon our lives. To be of help I researched cancer symptoms and treatments, attended every event of the American Cancer Society and dedicated myself to cancer research, raising awareness and lending support to patients and survivors. I attended a summer cancer class for several weeks to learn more. My dedication inspired friends to become involved and I was soon chosen to be president of the Tino Cancer Society and a member of the American Cancer Society Youth Council. I led the club from a membership of five to 86 and treasured the solidarity: we were one team fighting one illness.

Additionally, I have been working as a Grant Commissioner for the Santa Clara County Youth Task Force operating under the County Board of Supervisors and the Human Rights Commission. Assessing the proposals for grants submitted by schools and communities I allocate support for selected resources and services. Along with other youth leaders, I also present research findings concerning teen issues to various audiences, strengthening the voice of youth in our communities.

I firmly believe leadership to be both an inherent and foremost talent of mine, one that I have developed and enhanced. I am proud of my proactive attitude towards life.

On a Personal Level

*** Answer the following questions based on the passage.**

1. Have you ever heard of Youth Task Force? Do you know what their functions are?

2. What are your personal qualities?

3. How would you describe yourself? What are your positive/negative points?

4. Are you presently involved with any extracurricular activities in your community?

5. Any tragic events in your life?

Exercise A:

*** Make sentences about yourself using the following expressions.**

a. was for me a distant menace:

b. had intruded upon our lives:

c. dedicated myself to:

d. treasured the solidarity:

Exercise B:

*** Define the following words in English.**

a. fundraisers:

b. choreographed:

c. prostate cancer:

d. symptoms and treatments:

e. inherent:

g. proactive attitude:

Exercise C:

* Write a short summary of the passage.

B The Wrestling Match

There were only 15 seconds left in the final period, and I was down by eight points. My opponent's constant beating definitely didn't help assuage the throbbing pain all over my body and especially in my head as I felt blood pulsate throughout my body. On top of that, different thoughts were harassing my mind, fighting for my attention. Voices were trying to call out to me. The team really needed this win. I knew my parents were out there watching me. The frustration was mounting, but I concentrated and focused in on what I had been taught, what I knew I had to do.

Then, I instinctively felt my opportunity come. If I stayed still, I would lose but at least it would be over faster. That wasn't an option. Fighting to the end, challenging myself to rise above the pressure, having an undying will… and taking risks. I walked off the mat with satisfaction glowing on my face. Some say wrestling is a savage sport, filled with pain. To them, I respond that pain is weakness leaving the body, and I proudly represent myself as a wrestler.

On a Personal Level

*** Answer the following questions based on the passage.**

1. What are your favorite sports?

2. How do you spend your free time? What do you usually do on weekends?

3. Can you describe the feeling of losing/winning the game?

4. Comment on the following expression: "pain is weakness leaving the body."

5. Would you consider wrestling as a savage sport?

Exercise A:

* **Make sentences about yourself using the following expressions.**

a. help assuage the throbbing pain:

b. were trying to call out to me:

Exercise B:

* **Define the following words in English.**

a. pulsate:

b. harassing

c mounting:

d. instinctively:

e. undying will:

f. savage sport:

Exercise C:

* Write a short summary of the passage.

C The Golden Opportunity

Risk-taking is my distinguishing quality. I never back down from a challenge. Had I backed down, I wouldn't have run against the extremely popular class president at the time when I got involved with student government. Taking risks has always seemed to benefit me somewhat, like when I joined the school's competitive wrestling team in my sophomore year. I wanted to take advantage of wrestling as a physically and mentally demanding sport that could teach me valuable life lessons. The coaches and wrestlers all thought I was crazy for joining the sport so late, but I made sure that I change their attitudes in time.

Another example was the student concert that I helped organize. During the performance, I had a saxophone solo, which I was considering skipping because the large crowd made me unsure of my abilities. When I heard the musical cue, though, I knew not playing wasn't an option. I let my passion overtake my fear as I belted out my own melody. It was scary diving in with so much passion without inhibitions, but this made me realize how gratifying it could be taking that chance when everybody complimented me on the beauty of my solo. Opportunities come and go, and I've got to be able to take a risk when the chance comes.

On a Personal Level

*** Answer the following questions based on the passage.**

1. Do you know how to play any musical instruments?

2. What genre of music do you enjoy listening to?

3. Do you go to the concert often?

4. Are you willing to take a risk when opportunity comes?

Exercise A:

*** Make sentences about yourself using the following expressions.**

a. back down from:

b. changed their attitudes in time:

c. let my passion overtake my fear:

d. opportunities come and go:

Exercise B:

*** Define the following words in English.**

a. inhibitions:

b. passion:

c. gratifying:

d. compliment

Exercise C:

*** Write a short summary of the passage.**

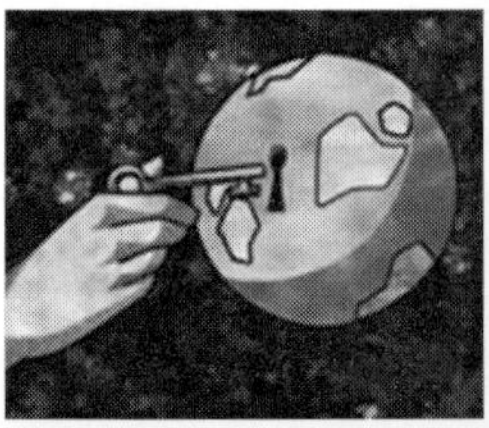

D The Tutoring Experience

Every time our eyes meet in the hallway, he comes up to me, playfully punching my shoulder, and I steal his baseball cap as we share a moment of male bonding. With a smile, he will tell me about all his little successes and failures that he had experienced recently in his life. After I give a few words of encouragement, we will part our ways, both more satisfied than before.

Tutoring kids through P. A. S. S. (Program for Achieving Scholastic Success) has been an unbelievably opportunity that I will forever look back upon with pride and smile. I have participated in a lot of groups helping the student body, but P. A. S. S. has been a unique opportunity that allows me to see, personally, the effects of my guidance and companionship on the troubled individuals in the program. P. A. S. S. was started by a group of teachers who had noted the unusually low grades among freshmen. They handpicked a few students to act as tutors for these students after school twice a week. I had always found immense satisfaction in tutoring someone and then watching him improve and exceed his own expectations. I jumped at the opportunity when my teacher came up to me with the proposal, and was initiated into this program. Through it, I was able to help two students, who were failing most of their classes, to get their grades up and gain confidence. I helped them sort through problems with friends and family, and even teachers, whom I boldly approached ever so often to ask how I could further help those kids. I desperately wanted to give these kids a second chance to succeed in both academics and their social life.

I was soon bringing in more and more of my friends to help tutor and guide these kids in P. A. S. S. In essence, I was quickly becoming a student leader in that program, but more importantly, I was becoming a leader in a few select individual's lives. Hand in hand, I was taking them towards the path to academic success and emotional stability. The position I had here was unlike any other leadership role I had at school. Sure, I could change people's social lives through my work in ASB and Band, but all those changes were trivial in comparison to the changes I was making for these misguided companions. Through that experience I matured so much in my ability to help others on a personal level, and I learned how to better constantly exude a positive, radiant aura that inspires optimism in others. The definition of a leader changed then for me. A leader can be found anywhere, be it in front of a large crowd at a rally, or be it simply in a small classroom talking one-on-one with another individual. Leaders lead, and that's exactly what I did with the students in P. A. S. S.

It's impossible for me to describe how I feel every time one of them comes up to me in the hallway and exclaims, "Hey James, guess what? I just got an A in math." Those smiles are proof enough that my efforts have made an ineffable difference.

On a Personal Level

*** Answer the following questions based on the passage.**

1. Have you ever tutor someone before? In what subject?

2. Were you a good tutor who made a difference on other people's academic performances?

3. Do we have a program similar to PASS in Korea?

4. Give a few words of encouragement to a student who is academically failing.

Exercise A:

* **Make sentences about yourself using the following expressions.**

a. share a moment of male bonding:

b. successes and failures that you have experienced recently:

c. immense satisfaction:

d. go give one a second chance to succeed:

Exercise B:

* **Define the following words in English.**

a. inhibitions:

b. troubled individuals:

c. handpicked:

d. hand in hand:

e. misguided companions:

f. exude a positive:

g. radiant aura:

Exercise C:

*** Write a short summary of the passage.**

E The Band Competition

Since starting high school two years ago, I have experienced a rapid succession of events in my life. One of them, which amounted to no more than ten minutes on the football field, always stands out in my mind and has changed my life significantly.

Our first competition of the year was the Tournament of the Bands. This competition has a time−honored tradition and is in fact the oldest high school band competition in California. We were the host band for this competition. I remember vividly the first moment we marched onto the field, when thousands of people who had paid to get in were wildly cheering. They had come to watch and hear us, they had come to watch and hear *me*, and they were a wild boisterous bunch. Scattered pockets of people in the crowd yelled out encouragement to specific names. However, we stood as still as the Queen's royal guards, not flinching or looking around. We were so still and the crowd clamored so hard that it seemed as if the plumes on our shakos were fluffing around on that windless night not because of the night breeze, but because of the undulating exuberance from the audience. In the confusion of uproar and hollering, there were two very loud and clear voices coming from the top of the judge's box. One was that of Rob, our marching instructor, who yelled out, "Play Loud!" The other was that of Mr. Harper, the band director, who screamed to us, "Perform!"

I held my cold steely saxophone with two hands, being too nervous even to quiver with edginess. The black plastic mouthpiece rested in my mouth, and I tasted the reed's distinct woody flavor. My sweaty fingers were starting to get slightly wet from the saliva and warm air seeping out of my finger pads. The football field had never loomed so immense and so imposing to me. I could see in the distance a multitude of the enthusiastic crowd. Their cheering and jubilation scared me more than encouraged me. A tingle of timidity ran down my back as I moved my eyes around and saw my fellow band-mates all standing at full and rigid attention. My knees were slightly cramped from standing up so straight for seemingly so long. I could feel my knuckles freezing. I began to worry that my fingers might lose the dexterity needed for a superior play.

Suddenly in that moment, I realized and felt the collective beauty and magnificence of our band. Those hundred brilliantly white plumes stood tall against the cool night sky, and I stood taller with my shoulders relaxed, my face emotionless, chin up, elbows out, chest up, and gripping harder than ever on my sax. I was ready to represent my school, and to play so hard that the crowd's hair would stand on end. I remembered the hundreds of hours we had spent rehearsing for this performance, and I promised myself that I would not let the band down, that I would not let the crowd down, and that I would not let down Mr. Harper and Rob with their huge smiling faces. Then, we started the show. I played my heart out and at the end I was practically dead from all the energy I had exerted in the performance and the music. I was exhausted, yet thrilled because I had just encountered an experience so surreal and transcendental that I had never encountered before. I felt how exhilarating it was to be part of a group and to work collectively for common accomplishment.

Those ten minutes on the field served as inspiration to my zealous devotion to playing saxophone. I gave up going out on the weekends preferring spending countless hours practicing saxophone and studying the drill book. During daily practices I was extremely serious in improving marching skills along with the rest of the band. My determination soon spread to the entire saxophone section. Our section quickly became a model group in the band. By the end of the first band season I had developed into an aspiring leader and skilled musician.

Those ten minutes have also made me realize that music is one of my passions as well. Even during off-season, I never stop playing saxophone. I play it whenever I find time. Playing music has become an integral part of my daily life. I will always remember those ten minutes out on the football field. Those ten minutes have enriched my life and changed my life, and have been my inspiration in high school.

On a Personal Level

*** Answer the following questions based on the passage.**

1. Have you ever entered any competitions in your life?

2. By reading the passage, can you feel the intensity aroused in the last ten minutes of the competition?

3. Have you ever involved with any team competitions?

4. Do you know the true meaning of the word, teamwork?

Exercise A:

* **Make sentences about yourself using the following expressions.**

a. yelled out encouragement to specific names:

b. the undulating exuberance from the audience:

c. too nervous even to quiver with edginess:

d. cheering and jubilation scared me more than encouraged me:

e. knees cramped from standing:

f. lose the dexterity:

g. play so hard that the crowd's hair would stand on end:

Exercise B:

*** Define the following words in English.**

a. boisterous bunch:

b. plumes:

c. uproar:

d. loomed:

e. timidity:

f. surreal:

g. exhilarating:

Exercise C:

*** Write a short summary of the passage.**

F The Spirit Committee

I had always wished to participate in my student class council. Yet once I had received a position I realized the true superficiality and corruptness that the council had woven into what they portrayed to be leadership and camaraderie. I believe that human nature is susceptible to corruption but that temptation does not excuse wrongdoing. Undermining an individual for personal gain is unnecessary and I now know that it is possible to achieve success without contemptuous methods.

I truly realized how ruthless people can become during homecoming week. It was as if a disease had overcome the entire council: they were obsessed with our competitors, earning points, and painting posters. During the canned food drive for the Second Harvest Food Bank, the worst display of despicable behavior was actually seen in my friend, the class president. Spirit points' were presented as a reward for the class who collected the most cans. In response, my friend deceived the underclassmen, creating the illusion that our class had no cans. On the last day of the drive, the council brought in 2,000 plus cans all at once. The underclassmen were in a state of complete shock and anger at the unfair display of senior pride. As my friend sighed in her undeserving satisfaction, her actions defeated the entire purpose of the drive: helping families in need. It was at that point, I decided I would not allow myself to compromise my morals for what amounted to simple vanity.

When I first became a part of the Spirit Committee, I was thrilled at finally obtaining a voice in the class council and participating in an active role. As a member, I learned how to balance my academics and extracurricular activities efficiently as well as develop leadership skills and organization. Most importantly, I learned that, although a group of people may unite together for a common goal, their true intent may be to further themselves. I carry pride in my ability to maintain my self-worth and morals instead of conforming to such selfish behavior. I believe that true success is composed of a justified merit and an altruistic fervor. I am fully aware that journalism, the career I plan to seek, is exposed to a highly competitive surrounding of potentially questionable motives and objectives; regardless, I will continue to align my ambitions with my morals as I pursue both my studies and my career.

On a Personal Level

*** Answer the following questions based on the passage.**

1. Do you know what canned-food-drive is?

2. Have you ever involved with extracurricular activities in your school?

3. Illustrate the following sentence: "I believe that human nature is susceptible to corruption but that temptation does not excuse wrongdoing."

Exercise A:

*** Make sentences about yourself using the following expressions.**

a. to achieve success without contemptuous methods:

b. to compromise my morals:

c. obtaining a voice in the class council:

d. to align my ambitions with my morals:

Exercise B:

*** Define the following words in English.**

a. ruthless:

b. despicable behavior:

c. vanity:

d. altruistic:

e. fervor

Exercise C:

*** Write a short summary of the passage.**

IV
DIVERSE PROGRAMS

A. Joint Programs

B. Life on Campus

C. Personalized Classes

D. The Flexible Curriculum

E. Undergraduate Seminars

A Joint Programs

It is a given that technology is a vital part of our society that, inevitably, keeps evolving as time advances. To this extent, it is imperative that corporations not only accept this ineluctable change, but embrace it and use it to their advantage. With this in mind, I believe that, because the program in management and technology is built around the boundary between management and technology, this program will help me in my ultimate goal of becoming an entrepreneur in the bioengineering field. My strong interests in both management and engineering are the driving forces underlying my desire to apply for this program.

This program will provide me with the best education in management as well as in engineering. Knowledge in both of these fields is crucial to an aspiring businessman in today's society. In addition, my classmates in this program will undoubtedly make up a phenomenal pool of talents whom I look forward both to cooperating with and competing against. The presence of such potential also means that I will have access to an amazing network that will surely help propel my career aspirations. Furthermore, the prestige of this program and the quality of education that it offers will certainly help me find top–notch internships during and after my studies and contribute to building my portfolio for admission to a top MBA program.

Engineering is something I will be successful with because it plays to my academic strengths: math and science. I have always excelled at math given the fact that I finished Calculus BC as a sophomore and, since then, have taken Linear Algebra and Multivariable Calculus. I have been an active participant in my school's math club. My success in math competitions shows in my qualification for AIME tests twice, both times scoring above the national average. I have also always excelled and pushed myself in science. Sophomore year I found that my Chemistry Honors class was not challenging enough. So I studied Chemistry AP in my free time and ended up scoring a 5 on the Chemistry AP test. Through my studies, I have also become intrigued with the ingenuity of mathematical proofs and the intricacies of chemical reactions and biological functions. With this interest and ability in math and science, engineering is a career choice that fits me naturally.

My interest in management stems from the leadership roles I have been in since I became involved with the student council in middle school. My interest in leadership and management has since grown to rival my interest in engineering. I was elected Class President in my sophomore year. In my junior year I was elected Student Body Vice President, and in the senior year I was selected to the Student Body Executive Council. I have full confidence in my ability to lead and manage an organization in the future and I will enjoy doing so as well.

The program will definitely be a challenging experience, but I am sure I am up to the task, since I have always challenged myself. At the same time, this program will be a valuable enriching and rewarding experience.

Point of View

*** Answer the following questions based on the passage.**

1. Are you utilizing the joint programs at your school?

2. What two academic areas are you interested?

3. How have you been preparing for joint programs?

Exercise A:

*** Make sentences about yourself using the following expressions.**

a. built around the boundary between:

b. ultimate goal of becoming an entrepreneur:

c. will undoubtedly make up a phenomenal pool of talents:

d. will surely help propel my career aspirations:

Exercise B:

*** Define the following words in English.**

a. ineluctable change:

b. prestige:

c. intrigued:

d. ingenuity:

e. intricacies:

Exercise C:

* Write a short summary of the passage.

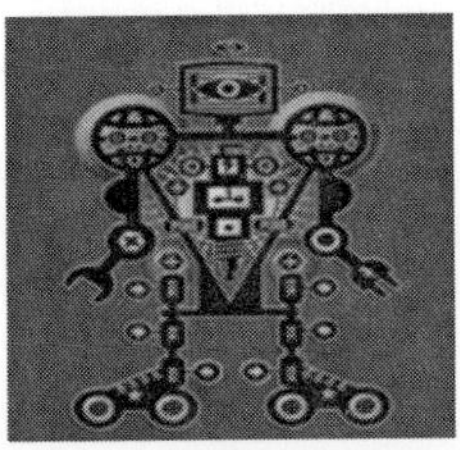

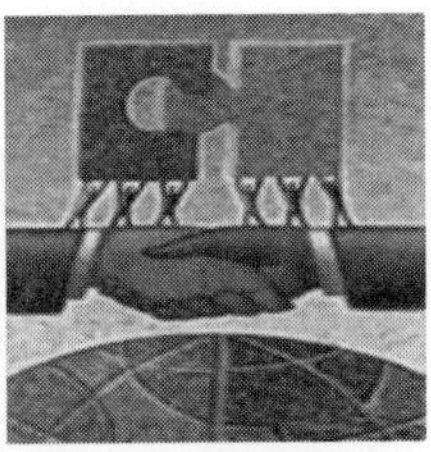

B Life on Campus

Take a stroll down University street. Any walker there will pass countless bikers and runners, young students playing soccer on the freshly mown grass and a host of sports facilities. This quiet urban neighbourhood is infused with a soothing aura despite being a seat of pride and power. The university offers exceptional qualities perfectly suited to my personality, my interests and my future designs for my life. Being a competitive athlete and student, I want to attend a college that is prideful of its achievements and scholars. Furthermore, the contrasting atmospheres – the one charged, the other comforting – complement each other to create a perfect campus for sociable, motivated individuals like me.

Throughout high school I was able to maintain a good balance between my academic and social lives. The university offers many extra–curricular opportunities that will enable me to find an equal balance of academics and outside interests. Whether fountain–hopping with friends, marching at the stadium with my flute or observing bacteria plates at the science laboratory, I will be able to enjoy a full life, working hard and playing hard.

The diversity of students creates university's unique, home-grown traditions as well as influencing the culture of the school. I am thrilled that the university is also one of the few schools in the nation that offers research opportunities and medical training, such as at the Epilepsy Center, to its undergraduate students. Certainly, with its academic standards, nurturing environment and diverse student body, university will give me the freedom to learn, teach, compete and socialize. Walking in to campus, I will feel the wind of freedom blowing.

Point of View

*** Answer the following questions based on the passage.**

1. Do you enjoy your campus life?

2. How does campus life in high school different from college?

3. Describe your campus atmosphere during spring and fall.

4. What is your favorite season on campus?

Exercise A:

* **Make sentences about yourself using the following expressions.**

a. is infused with a soothing aura:

b. future designs for my life:

c. nurturing environment:

d. feel the wind of freedom blowing:

Exercise B:

*** Define the following words in English.**

a. diversity:

b. epilepsy:

c. suburban:

Exercise C:

*** Write a short summary of the passage.**

C Personalized Classes

Waiting for him in the classroom, a thrill of anticipation ran through me. To occupy myself I doodled lists on my notepad. Then suddenly in walked the man we had been waiting for, Dr. Richard Jones.

He began the class immediately, showing myself and my fellow biotechnology students a video clip of a patient suffering a bout of epilepsy. Grabbing and holding my interest from the start, Dr. Jones proceeded with explanations of neuro-related diseases. Epilepsy and Alzheimer's are the consequences of imbalances in the nervous system, aberrations evident in the simple yet informative pictures of the human brain that Dr. Jones displayed.

In addition to his lecture, Dr. Jones presented demonstrations of neurological practices, using student volunteers and an array of equipment. I was called on to help with blind eye mapping, a process unfamiliar to me. The doctor held out a thin wire with a red circular sticker attached at one end. When he set the wire at a certain angle, the red dot disappeared from my view. However, after a minor, barely perceptible adjustment, the dot was again visible. Dr. Jones' demonstrations intrigued me and, after witnessing the quick reflexes of the human brain and the effects of neurological stimulation, I walked away astonished.

The cancer course of Education Program has allowed me to use university's medical facilities and kept me informed about research opportunities on campus. Instructive as these opportunities have been, I found the two hours with Dr Jones more captivating and entertaining. Through simple demonstrations and comprehensive explanations about nervous systems, I now possess an abiding interest that I will likely pursue in college.

Point of View

*** Answer the following questions based on the passage.**

1. Have you ever taken any summer programs before?

2. What research programs are available at your university?

3. Do you have any concerns over any incurable diseases such as cancer and epilepsy?

Exercise A:

*** Make sentences about yourself using the following expressions.**

a. to occupy myself I doodled lists:

b. was called on to help with:

c. walked away astonished:

d. possess an abiding interest:

Exercise B:

*** Define the following words in English.**

a. biotechnology:

b. neuro-related diseases:

c. perceptible adjustment:

d. stimulation:

e. captivating:

Exercise C:

* **Write a short summary of the passage.**

D The Flexible Curriculum

The college I seek will have a rigorous but flexible academic curriculum complemented by a rich variety of social activities, thereby creating a stimulating and yet enjoyable environment. The university possesses numerous attributes that make it the ideal match for my academic and social interests.

For me, the most appealing asset of the university is its abundance of undergraduate research opportunities. I have a strong desire for a college that provides a rich supply of resources and welcomes curiosity.

More specifically, I seek a learning institute that encourages academic rigor as well as interaction between students through undergraduate research projects. At the university, the faculty's generosity to students, by assisting discussion groups with the selection and analysis of research papers, is particularly impressive. Research programs enable students to acquaint themselves with the diverse genres of science. My participation in programs such as the Biological Basis of Behavior Program will enable me to develop my interests and explore the boundless field of neurology. Research of social behaviors of organisms or developments of the human body's sensory systems will enhance my knowledge of neurology.

University is a natural and compelling match for me precisely because of its scientific research programs as well as the availability of research grants for undergraduates. As a prospective University of Pennsylvania student, I aspire to participate in cutting-edge science research, if opportunity allows.

The university's unique academic programs such as interdisciplinary learning available for undergraduates are similarly enticing. Throughout my high school years, I was interested in a wide spectrum of different disciplines, from business to science. At the university I would have the choice of taking a dual-degree path in any combination of two disciplines. I am also attracted to the special joint degree programs that integrate courses from two different colleges, enabling students to express their academic creativity and increase the depth of understanding in two different disciplines.

Opportunities for international study through university abroad program are appealing also. Organizing programs and advising students about studying abroad as well as sampling the world's various cultures will profit me academically and reward me personally. My exposure to international academic resources will help imbue me with a global academic sensibility.

Academia aside, there are many residential programs that encourage non-academic interests and hobbies. I have always believed in a balance between study and social activities. These residential programs will provide me a chance to explore music and other hobbies of mine.

Point of View

*** Answer the following questions based on the passage.**

1. Do you have abroad programs available at your university?

2. What residential programs do you carry at your university.

3. Do you know what joint degree programs are? Do you have any research grants available for undergraduate students at your university?

4. What characteristics would you consider the most important in choosing a college?

Exercise A:

* **Make sentences about yourself using the following expressions.**

a. creating a stimulating and yet enjoyable environment:

b. the most appealing asset of the university is:

c. provides a rich supply of resources and welcomes curiosity:

d. to acquaint themselves with the diverse genres of science:

e. to explore the boundless field of neurology:

f. will enhance my knowledge:

g. enabling students to express their academic creativity:

h. sampling the world's various cultures:

Exercise B:

*** Define the following words in English.**

a. rigorous but flexible:

b. academic rigor:

c. cutting-edge science:

d. interdisciplinary:

e. a wide spectrum of different disciplines:

Exercise C:

*** Write a short summary of the passage.**

E Undergraduate Seminars

First off, the seminars at the university seem extremely thought-provoking, especially for freshmen. As a freshman, I would love to take a course that boasted eye-opening experiences and fascinating discussions, which is what the seminars seem to center on. These seminars seem like a chance to explore a subject deeply as a freshman, increasing interest and passion to learn more about the subject.

The second reason why I am interested in this course is that I have a strong interest in management. I have served in a leadership role in numerous activities in my high school career, including in city government, student government, marching band, wrestling and tennis, and with these experiences my interest in management and leadership has rapidly grown. Because the roles I have had in high school center more on human interactions and human resource management, I am more specifically interested in the field of human resource management, and recognize that human labor and the management of human resources are the most important components in any organization.

During the summer before my senior year in high school, I even served as a Human Resource intern. Because the management department was relatively small, I played a key role in many aspects of the Human Resource department which has further piqued my interest in this field. That is why this freshman seminar in Human Resource seems like something that is certainly worth exploring to me.

Point of View

* **Answer the following questions based on the passage.**

1. Have you ever utilized the internship programs at your university?

2. What internship programs are available at your school?

Exercise A:

*** Make sentences about yourself using the following expressions.**

a. seem extremely thought-provoking:

b. to take a course that boasted eye-opening experiences:

c. has further piqued my interest:

Exercise B:

*** Define the following words in English.**

a. piqued:

b: human resource management:

Exercise C:

* Write a short summary of the passage.

V
FIELD OF STUDY

A. Rubik's Cube

B. Chosen Career

C. Personal Interests

A Rubik's Cube

Christmas 2006. Wrapped tightly in a blanket, I rushed down the hall to the living room. The Christmas tree stood proud, adorned in golden lights and red ornaments. With sleepy eyes, I hunted for my Christmas present. My heart pounded faster and faster as I tossed neatly-wrapped boxes aside. Ah, found it! I ripped open the red wrapping paper and… found nothing but a Rubik's cube.

A Rubik's cube with instructions to solve it. Discarding the instructions, I stared at the six-colored cube. I turned right, then down. I had always enjoyed solving riddles, but this cube was a tough one. This small, multicolored enigma grabbed, and then held, my attention. Solving the cube was apparently impossible, yet I still twisted and turned the sides…

Science is an infinite puzzle with missing pieces. The unknowns outweigh the knowns, and in its persistent search for answers, mankind has yet to solve many of the questions.

Last summer, under the support of the education program, I took a cancer research course at the university. Invited to examine research papers on any topic, I chose to research survivin, a drug resistance that inhibits apoptosis, especially in tumor-associated endothelial cells. My detailed study of the human brain and its endothelial cells fuelled an interest in neurology and the mysterious workings of the nervous system. Through this, I foresaw a vision of my future, an extension of my passion for science.

I seek a college that provides a rich supply of resources and welcomes curiosity. More specifically, I am looking for a learning institute that encourages academic rigor as well as interaction between students through undergraduate research projects. Your university is a natural and compelling match for me precisely because of its scientific research and clubs. The faculty's generosity to students, by assisting discussion groups with the selection and analysis of research papers, is particularly impressive. Research clubs enable students to acquaint themselves with the diverse genres of science. My participation in clubs such as neurobiology club for undergraduates will enable me to develop my interests and explore the boundless field of neurology.

As a prospective college student, I aspire to serve

groundbreaking research. Research of social behaviors of organisms or developments of the human body's sensory systems, under the guidance of professors such as Dr. David Smithson, will enhance my knowledge of neurology to the point that I may help unravel any given project's riddle.

February 2007. Click. I have finally solved the 3x3x3, leaving me yearning for a 4x4x4. Although I have solved a small mystery, no one will ever find the answers to all of science's mysteries; one answer will lead to another question, which will encounter an answer that sparks another mystery. This, for me, is the fascination of science.

Reading Comprehension

*** Answer the following questions.**

1. Do you know how to solve Rubik's cube?

2. Are you presently involved with any clubs on campus?

3. What was your motivation of choosing your field of study?

4. Are you satisfied with your major?

B The Chosen Career

Journalism and writing itself is my most fervent passion. Although I have only been in journalism for two years in my high school career, it has given me entirely new perspectives in the writing world. I feel that journalism is one of the greatest remaining and continuing influences upon people. With writing, comes the ability to influence the thoughts and opinions of others as well as convey new perspectives. In this manner, a writer is able to express his or her opinions, thoughts, and emotions to readers. When a newspaper becomes a reliable and trustworthy source, readers will look towards it for guidance and actually want to read the opinions and perspectives on current events. I want to develop and pursue this author–audience relationship in the world of journalism and express my ideas through this communication and literary freedom.

Through journalism I hope to build many bridges and relationships with new people as I further enhance my communication abilities. I am a highly sociable and gregarious person, hence I love to work with others, discussing topics and simply interacting with them in general. I am no longer confined by the format of essays, but given the opportunity to write my opinions and thoughts as I wish. I love the freedom journalism gives, allowing me to stretch and further develop my mind, creating entire new worlds and perspectives. The power to influence, to inform, and to share all comes through journalism and I believe that it is an utmost necessity to utilize and polish these abilities. In my future journalistic academics, I wish to achieve a sense of maturity in my writing eloquence and articulation as well as obtain the ability to effortlessly transfer my thoughts unto paper. And with these aspects of effective communication and a well-developed writing ability, I want to perfect the expression of my thoughts and opinions in a universal way, appealing to readers in an eye-opening-attention-grabbing manner. It is one concept to be able to capture a thought and physically put it unto paper, but an entirely another to be able to adequately communicate the thought to the people.

I do realize that the world of journalism is one of the most competitive careers, filled with brilliant and sharp writers along with fierce ambitions; but I genuinely and whole-heartedly long to become a part of this world. Writing is the source of information people seek, an escape from everyday life, the second opinion and new perspective; it is what enriches the mind and feeds the soul; and it is through the power and source of journalism that this may be communicated to the people. I hope to pursue my writing future in the field of journalism at the exemplary the university where I will refine my writing skills and expand my literary perspectives along with the clarity of communication in my future written works.

Reading Comprehension

*** Answer the following questions.**

1. Define the world of journalism.

2. What prospective jobs can you get from majoring in journalism?

3. In order to be a professional journalist, what personal qualities are required?

C Personal Interests

During my high school years, I have developed quite heterogeneous interests in a variety of disciplines, among which business and bioengineering have emerged to be my passion. I have hence decided to pursue a career involving both these interests. During my college and post-graduate academic years, I plan to develop a master understanding of the rapidly growing bioengineering field and to gain full knowledge of business by studying for an MBA degree.

It is a given that technology permeates society and will inevitably keep evolving as time advances. In turn, society will forever be insatiable for advanced technology. Therefore, it is imperative that corporations not only recognize ineluctable technological changes, but embrace them and take full advantage of them. Equipped with an MBA degree and an understanding of the bioengineering field, I hope to become a successful entrepreneur in that field. Knowledge in both business and bioengineering will be crucial in order for me to keep up with all the new self-reinforcing technological advancements at the time as well as to create and market any innovations that I may come up with.

Not all entrepreneurs are successful in the history of business, but out of every batch there are a limited few that come up with new inventions that would revolutionize society. I aspire to be one of the few who can create and market a technology that will extend human capabilities and bring positive impact on society. This is not an easy goal to accomplish, but I believe that just being able to recognize that fact takes me one step closer to bringing my dreams to fruition. I might be shooting for the moon, but as the saying goes, even if I miss, at least I'll land amongst the stars that shine on humanity.

Reading Comprehension

*** Answer the following questions.**

1. Define the field of bioengineering.

2. What is MBA degree?

3. Is your major suits well with your interest?

VI
VARIETY TOPICS

A. Roommates

B. Classes to Remember

C. The Deeper Meaning of Life

D. Traveling

E. Extracurricular Activities

F. My Room

G. The Park

H. A Parent Letter

A Roommates

I am a package of spontaneity, generosity, competitiveness, and compassion. However, I cannot claim to be the perfect roommate. I may sometimes be too confident, work-oriented, and overly talkative. I adore listening to music, varying from hardcore rap to soft jazz. Also, I am extremely active in school activities. I help boost my high school class' spirit and pride by organizing fundraisers, cheers, and social events. Basketball is a huge piece of my life; I played point guard for my school and cheered for the Varsity boys at every home game until I lost my voice. I also love to dance, though I have yet to pursue my talents and interests in it. I have choreographed the Class of 2009 girls' homecoming dance every year. I think dancing is a way to relieve stress and express my feelings. Besides that, I like to play any type of sports, take care of my little cousins, volunteer at community events and hospitals, teach math to children, spread cancer awareness, and watch Animal Planet and "Snapped" on Oxygen.

More importantly, I become easily inspired, and I tend to take action with that inspiration. I have built many interests through my motivation to pursue those inspirations. For example, cancer has indirectly impacted my life in significant ways; consequently, I am now passionate about spreading awareness of cancer. I have upgraded an inactive club, Tino Cancer Society, into a 70+ member club this year. I have never felt more accomplished when I saw the sign-up list. Hopefully, the club will make noticeable changes on our campus through projects such as distributions of cookbooks to promote healthy eating, participation in Relay for Life, and distributions of colored ribbons.

I am thrilled for college life, to live on my own and pursue my interests in a higher-level education. Hopefully, we share common interests and ideas, that way we can make our time at the university a fun, inspiring experience.

Thoughts and Opinions

*** Answer the following questions.**

1. Tell us about your roommates.

2. Do share common interests with your roommates?

3. What do you usually do with your roommates?

B Classes to Remember

World Core, which is a combination of World Literature and World History, has definitely been the most rewarding class I've taken this year. I have learned the teachings and ideas of many prominent philosophers throughout history such as Plato, John Locke, and Thomas Hobbes. I have also read many books written by authors from other countries such as *In the Time of the Butterflies*, *For Whom the Bell Tolls*, and *Dawn*. I also understand many of the different governments from the past and present, and have studied revolutions and why they occur. I can now read the newspaper and know where the different countries around the globe are and am able to analyze international matters more carefully through this course.

I would like to study Statistics and Writing. I have a very strong interest in math and am quite skilled in it. Because of budget cuts, our school unfortunately had to cut AP Statistics from the curriculum, so I'd like to study it at Harvard. I want to study Writing as well because I think writing well is extremely important because communication is key to almost everything.

The most interesting book I've read in the past year is *Cry, The Beloved Country*. It was an extremely touching book because it was so sad yet written in a way that made it extremely believable. I have learned about South Africa and its history of apartheid, so this really stuck to me. The history of South Africa amazes me, and this book really showed how sad it could be.

Thoughts and Opinions

*** Answer the following questions.**

1. What classes do you still remember from your high school?

2. What were your favorite/unfavorite classes?

3. Any particular book you've read in your high school years that still stays in your mind?

C The Deeper Meaning of Life

What is the meaning of life? The question that always plagues everyone's minds cannot be easily answered. Many spend their whole life finding an answer, because there has to be some meaning to life, or else why would we be here? I disagree. There is no answer to this perpetual and elusive question. One could ask, "What is life?" To this question, I would answer that it is the state of being alive: thinking, breathing, and eating. Or perhaps one might ask, "Why are we here?" I would answer that our existence is due to a series of whimsical evolutionary processes. Another question might be "Why do we live?" or "What is our purpose?" Being homo sapiens with a civilized society, we do not just live to reproduce and extend our legacy on Earth, which is what all other animals do. I believe this will to survive and propagate is replaced with something else altogether.

My answer can be found in Albert Camus' novel, *The Stranger*. Meursault is a man devoid of all emotions because he believes that life has no meaning, and that he should not waste effort being emotional. However, at the end of the novel, his mind happens upon a revelation: although life may not have any meaning, nevertheless he should enjoy the time he spends being alive. He realizes right before his execution that, due to society's inability to accept his different personality, even if he is not accepted for his ideas and even if everyone reaches the same destination at the end of their lives, he is proud of being himself and proud of having pursued things his own way.

Meursault is an absurd hero, because his philosophy that in the big picture life is meaningless and that there is nothing after death is not accepted by society. Perhaps buying into his idea makes me an absurd hero as well. However, if anyone asks me "What is the meaning of life?" I will keep answering that there is no meaning to life. That not withstanding, we should pursue what makes us happy and what makes us unique.

Thoughts and Opinions

*** Answer the following questions.**

1. What would you like to accomplish throughout your life?

2. What is the true meaning of life in your opinion?

3. Do you know who Albert Camus is?

D Traveling

From sunbathing on the beaches of the Bahamas to riding canal in Venice, there are many hot spots around the world that travelers swarm to for vacations. None of these hot spots, however, is where I want to go. Rather than visit hot spots and enjoy the excitement and luxury, I would be more inclined to taste a calm, yet rugged, life in a small village called Tangwan in the remote rustic countryside of China.

Everyday, people are scrambling around doing their jobs without much time for just relaxing and enjoying the world around them. Even when people are on vacations, they have to worry about visiting certain places and waiting in line, or remembering to keep their passports in a safe place and catching flights early in the morning. In the countryside, all these worries are washed away because no one's ever yelling at you to get up in the morning, no one's ever fussing about you not working, and you can do things at your own pace. People in Tangwan are quite friendly, rather than the stiff ticket collectors that "greet" you at the entrance to a museum.

I visited Tangwan last summer. The beautiful scenery and the idyllic life there have ever been beckoning me back. There are lush green mountains with thousands of surrounding trees, and the streams are crystal clear without any pollutants in them. The melodious songs sung by the birds are soothing, and they are totally unbroken because there are no cars or other noisemakers to scare the birds away.

During my last visit, upon my arrival in the pastoral village Tangwan, I watched my uncle killing and gutting a chicken. Captivated by the dexterity with which he fastidiously preserved the edibles of the entrails and threw away the excrement, I stood by fascinated, following his every skillful movement with my devouring eyes. I then also saw some chickens. There was a large hen leading a group of about fifteen small chicks around the backyard, rooting and pecking for food. The chicks were like little soldiers in a single file, marching around, and quickly scattering at the slightest hint of threat. Sometimes they dispersed into a jungle of corn, but always emerged alive and together. Later on, I also saw some cute small pigs in a pig pen and was astounded at the tiny size of them. Those pigs were probably as small as big bunnies. My cousin and I found infinite pleasure in hand–feeding them with corn husks and small pieces of apples, our palms tingling with wetness and warmth from the pigs' snouts. I walked around the pigsties some more and encountered a humongous pig. This pig was as big as a cow, and probably weighed more than a ton.

During the three-day visit, I climbed mountains, made bows and arrows, and ran into many other amazing surprises. I found myself relieved of all stress modern society tends to impose on us and I was totally blended with nature there and then. Every morning I could breathe the cool fresh mountain air or appreciate the wonderful art of killing a chicken. I took baths in the cool mountain spring water and ran around the mountains exploring anything that was interesting. I absolutely loved my short stay there in the small village. And what would I not give in the world to visit it again?

Thoughts and Opinions

*** Answer the following questions.**

1. Have you been traveling abroad before?

2. Have you ever visited any place similar to China?

3. If opportunity allows, where would you like to go?

E Extracurricular Activities

The two activities that I have been involved the most with during the past four years have been marching band and Associate Student Body (ASB). I have held leadership positions in both these organizations for three years each. In band I have been the section leader of the Saxophones ever since my sophomore year and also founded Band Club, an effort to strengthen the connection between band and ASB. In ASB, I have served as Class President, ASB Spirit Commissioner, and ASB Vice President.

Whenever I think of my leadership in marching band, my mind goes back to one defining memory in my sophomore year. At a night practice, the band did a drill on horn movements. That being my first year as section leader, I was nervous about whether I had adequately prepared my section. My question was answered the second our director called the band to attention. All the saxophones snapped their horns up with remarkable precision. The director immediately looked towards us in shock, saying that my section had just shown a remarkable sense of pride and cohesion. That recognition inspired me to try even harder to improve my section. As a senior, I have had the opportunity to work with countless additions to the saxophone section and mold them to perfection, making the saxophones indisputably the best section in our band.

As part of ASB I have also made certain contributions that hopefully will leave a legacy. From experiences with other organizations, I realized our ASB needed a mission statement to focus in on every year, so I helped create one that emphasized student excitement. Branching off of that idea, I expanded on existing activities at school. For our school's Spirit Week, I recreated the guidelines to lengthen each day's activities from a half to a full day. It was a lot of work getting people to buy into this idea, but once I had general approval, I was able to improve an already outstanding school tradition. Currently, I am in the process of planning a city-wide carnival at my high school. I recognize the importance of delegation and involving people with varying talents, so I have enlisted the help of the city council, other ASB officers, and am currently looking for corporate sponsors. With all the experience I have had through ASB, I know I can make this carnival succeed as well.

As a leader in both band and ASB, I was inspired to create a stronger connection between the two, and have found ways to involve both in many student activities.

For example, there is now a pep band playing tunes at most student functions. Also, I founded Band Club within the jurisdiction of ASB, so band can voice its concerns and participate more easily in all ASB activities.

I have found many opportunities to lead and make changes in high school. Through my experiences, I have attained leadership and teamwork skills, as well as a confidence in my ability to make a difference.

Throughout my high school years, I have become interested in a number of different disciplines, including business and bio-engineering. I wish to pursue a career involving both of these interests. During my graduate and post-graduate academic career, I wish to develop an understanding of the rapidly growing bio-engineering field, as well as study for an MBA.

It is a given that technology is a vital part of our society that, inevitably, keeps evolving as time advances. To this extent, it is imperative that corporations not only accept this ineluctable change, but embrace it and use it to their advantage. Armed with an MBA and an understanding of the bio-engineering field, I hope to become a successful entrepreneur in that field. Knowledge in both business management as well as bio-engineering will be crucial in order for me to keep up with all the new technological advancements at the time as well as create and market any innovation that I may come up with, and my education will allow me empower me with this knowledge.

There are very few entrepreneurs that are successful, but out of every batch there is at least one that comes up with a new invention that revolutionizes society and its technology. I aspire to be that one successful businessman who can create and market a revolutionary piece of science and improve society. This is not an easy goal to accomplish, but I believe that just being able to recognize that fact brings me one step closer to bringing my goals to fruition. I might be shooting for the moon, but as the saying goes, even if I miss, at least I'll land amongst the stars.

Thoughts and Opinions

*** Answer the following questions.**

1. Why did you choose your major as English Education?

2. Did you do anything to prepare for your major?

3. What kind of teacher would you like to be in the future?

F My Room

In some way, all objects in a room provide revelation of the occupant's character. Some people even go so far as to believe that one can be read by the items and layout of his or her room. In my room, everything is special to me, yet there is that one item that stands out of the crowd. That object is my saxophone.

Ever since I accidentally picked the saxophone as my musical instrument in band in sixth grade, I've learned to love it and have become very good at it. Seeing my rapid progress in sax playing, my dad bought me a brand new saxophone towards the end of my sixth grade. I played it everyday, and it became part of my life. Whenever I finish playing, I set it down on the bookshelf across from my bed. The case never gets dusty and the saxophone is always as good as new, because I always take the time to clean and care for it every few weeks. I always care for things as special as that, and make sure that everything is in great condition.

Whenever I sit down and just stare at that saxophone, I

think back to my first field show with the my high school marching band. The unforgettable details of my first show with my saxophone remain vivid in my mind whenever I see my saxophone in my room:

When we were readying ourselves in the field, thousands of people were wildly cheering, almost like a war cry. Scattered groups of people yelled out encouragement at us. Chunks of tasty nachos and juicy hot dogs were flying in the air. However, we stood as still as the Queen's royal guards without flinching or stirring. We were so still and the crowd cheered so hard that it seemed as if the plumes on our shakos were fluffing from the wind created by loud cheering. In this mixed confusion of noise, two clear voices were ringing in our ear. One was that of Rob, CHS' marching instructor, who yelled out, "Play Loud!" The other belonged to Mr. Harper, the band director, who shouted, "Perform!"

Thousands of salmon colored blotches dotted the bleachers on both sides of the field. On the field there were a hundred plumes and instruments in straight rows and columns. Then there were a lot of flags and dancers in red dresses in front of the hundred plumes. The bright, dazzling colors contrasted so much that one could go color−blind. On the front sideline was a podium, with our drum major in her green dress standing on it.

As a new member of the band, I held my cold

saxophone with my two hands, being too nervous even to quiver with nervousness. The black plastic mouthpiece rested in my mouth. I tasted the reed's distinct woody flavor. My sweaty fingers were starting to get wet from the saliva and warm air seeping out of my finger pads. All I could see in front of me was a multitude of people. Their cheering and yelling served more of a scare than encouragement to me. My well–polished saxophone glittered, alongside all the other shining instruments. All around me were my band mates standing at absolute attention. My knees were slightly cramped from standing up too straight for too long. I could feel my knuckles freezing, giving me the dread of their not being able to move fast enough for the performance. I could smell the now familiar odor of salty sweat in my shako and the musty smell of my wool uniform. In the cool breeze there was also a gentle waft of meaty hot dogs.

In that moment I realized our hundred brilliantly white plumes, standing tall against the cool nighttime breeze. I stood up taller, with my shoulders relaxed, my face emotionless, chin up, elbows out, chest up, gripping harder than ever on my sax. At that tense moment, I felt more challenged and overwhelmed than ever, but I was ready to represent my high school. I was ready to play so hard that the crowd's hair would stand on end. I remembered the hundreds of hours we had spent rehearsing for this show and I promised myself that I would not let the band down. Then we started the show. I played my heart out. I played my heart out. At the end, I was practically dead from all the energy I put in the show through my cool gold saxophone. I honored CHS Marching Band with my perfect performance!

My saxophone will forever be the key to go back and relive that one field show. When people walk into my room and see the saxophone, they'll notice that it's so clean and has been endowed with so much love and care that it almost glows compared to its dusty surroundings. That saxophone case with a sticker saying CHS Marching Band on the front shows my pride and passion for the things I really care about: the band and the saxophone.

Thoughts and Opinions

1. What items in your room do you adore the most?

2. What things in your room that will bring you a good memory into your mind?

3. Do you have anything that are specifically related to your high school days in a special way?

G The Park

In the distance, I can barely make out the dim glow of an old lamppost. Hurriedly, I run over to my landmark. I turn to my left, and carefully open the short metal gate, fearful of making any squeaks despite my certainty that no one is nearby. I loop around the merry go round, jump over the baby swings, and sprint up the short hill. There are stairs nearby, but naturally I chose not to take them. How am I going to experience life if every time I choose to take a boring path already laid out by others? Shivers run down my back as the chilly air creeps in my clothes, helping to clear some of frustration hazing my mind. Softly panting, I settle down on the hill's plateau on my behind Indian style.

I glance around and see the merry-go-round gently rocking back and forth in the wind. The baby swings are still unsettled from when I accidentally knocked them with the tip of my foot in my earlier unsuccessful jump. I let out a sigh. I can't seem to do anything right today. I guess I just need a minor adjustment in my leap next time. Minor adjustments. Darn it, sometimes it's just not easy to make certain adjustments. Unlike the swings, I can't redo the in-class essay that I bombed today with a minor adjustment in my posture. How can I reconcile my embarrassing loss at the tennis match today with just a "minor" adjustment? Sitting atop that plateau, I return to the worries, fears and anxieties I had throughout the day. I take another deep breath, and fall back to lie down on the plateau.

In the night sky of a city, one can rarely make out enough stars to form a constellation, but here I can easily locate the Big Dipper, as well as Orion's Belt, or at least, what I have come to convince myself to be the real Orion's belt amongst the numerous stars. As I stare up at the stars, my mind wanders to what I have done wrong. It was my lack of enough analysis that destroyed the focus of my in-class essay. My tennis loss was due to my inability to concentrate on each stroke rather than worry uselessly about the score. That's past though. I can't bog myself down by stressing and stewing over my mistakes. Now I just have to cool down, collect my senses, and accomplish my next goal. That in-class essay can be revenged with an amazing poetry analysis paper next week. My next tennis match will be controlled by my focused strokes. Everything in my mind becomes so much clearer as my eyes lose focus. Finally, content, I close my eyes.

Beep, beep, beep··· I slowly open my eyelids as I hear my watch's alarm telling me that it's getting late and it's time for me to leave. Reluctantly, I sit back up and brush the gravel from my back. I take my time walking down the slope of the hill, making sure to avoid the ordinary stairs, and take a last tour of the area. I gently slide my hands around the merry go round, until finally my fingers slip away as I walk through the gate. With one last glance back, I reflect on the numerous dilemmas that I've worked through in the peaceful silence there at night. Sometimes, I just need that bit of silence to prevent myself from despairing and to get my thoughts in order again. Despite the chilly winter breeze, I feel a sense of warmth deep down inside, stemming from the satisfaction that I have gained by trading away my anxiety and fear.

Softly, I tiptoe away from the playground and into the darkness.

Thoughts and Opinions

1. Have you ever stayed in a park in the dark?

2. What do you do to get your thoughts in order?

3. What personal problems do often encounter now days?

H A Parent Letter

Recently when I asked Robert about his school, he said that he could be more challenged and some classes could go faster. I said, "OK, I will send you to a place where you will be fully challenged!" That was how we first embarked on the search for the best educational program in the country, which led us to Phillips Academy. After some serious discussion, we decided that Robert apply to Academy for the best learning environment and the most challenging academic programs.

Robert is a very motivated and intelligent student. At the age of eight, he was identified as having an IQ of 160 by a Mensa intelligence test. He then participated in several gifted and talented youth programs. A strong love for learning, a great enthusiasm for knowledge, and a simple curiosity to learn for learning's sake put him in a relentless pursuit for academic challenge. And he has certainly excelled, especially in math and in languages. For example, as a first generation ABK (American Born Korean), Robert values Korean culture and language.

Although he never lived in a Korean–speaking community and only visited Korea once for five weeks, he made a tireless effort of learning the Korean language well. To our delight, he began to publish Korean essays in the most widely circulated Korean newspaper outside Korea, *The World Journal*, when he was nine. He has since published over twenty Korean essays and has won numerous Korean essay prizes, including the "Extraordinary Prize" in an International Korean Essay – Writing contest with six million participants all over the world, including native speakers in Korea.

Robert tries also to achieve a balance in all academic areas. For example, he knows that he is very strong in math. In order to balance out, when deciding on what extra courses to take for summers and for extra–curricular choices, he has often opted for writing courses and has successfully finished three college–challenging level writing courses. Over time, he has won so many awards, trophies, and honor rolls that we have lost count of them.

Not only strong in academics, Robert is also a good citizen. His is truly a heart of gold. Even since he was three or four years old, he somehow began to have a strong sense of protecting the environment and public goods. For example, he would express a strong uneasiness if he saw a tap dripping water or saw any litter in the public ground and would always have us fix the problems right there. He began to assume various student cabinet roles and community roles in his eighth grade. He values difference and diversity and has a strong sense of independence and responsibility.

One thing as a father I even admire in him is his magnanimity and equanimity in the face of adversity or defeat. Recently, Robert suffered two defeats, so to speak. One is that he was defeated by his friend Paul in running for the 9th grade president of the student cabinet and the other is that he had to abort his attempt in staying in the AP Calculus BC course. I asked him why he couldn't beat Paul. Instead of going into various excuses and extenuating circumstances, Robert simply answered, "Because Paul is a better person overall." When I asked him about his frustration in the Calculus BC course, he said, "Because I cannot skip Calculus A that easily." I was truly touched by his sincerity, modesty and philosophical attitudes towards these two issues.

When Robert decides to do something, he truly puts his heart to it. We see this in his involvement with the school math club, the school band, and the student government. We see this again in his work in the City Teen Commission's attempt in establishing a teen center. He always devotes himself to whatever is new, right, and positive. He understands that he has so much to learn and so much to contribute as well.

My letter may sound a bit boastful and biased. Of

course, I am a parent! Yet, I truly believe what I stated here is very true of my son. In fact, I grappled hard with how best I could characterize him and I believe no matter what I write, it may not do justice to a child so eager to learn, so anxious to excel, and so kind and loving in his heart! Robert is truly a parental pride!

What I want is, however, the absolute best educational environment and the absolutely most challenging academic programs. What I want is also Robert's even more accelerated pace of intellectual maturity, personal independence, and greater exposure to more diversified student body. And I think the Academy represents the best match for all of these desires.

The Academy is beyond doubt the quint essential American preparatory school with the longest and richest history of educating America's best students. It is a cradle of leadership and it provides absolutely the best environment for intellectual development. We are extremely impressed with the wide spectrum of curricular and extracurricular programs offered at the Academy, and we are particularly impressed with Academy's ability to attract the best and brightest students all over the world. We believe that Robert will blend very well into Academy's cultural and learning environments. We also believe that Robert will add to the diversity of Academy's student body and will contribute to Academy in terms of enriching the class with his cultural experience and understanding, with his integrity, kindness, and his perennial willingness to help. Robert will be proud of studying at Academy, and will no doubt make Academy proud of him in return. In short, we are ready to make Academy an inseparable part of Robert's incipient independent life, a life full of his own hopes and our expectations. Let knowledge, intellect, love, and kindness shine in him for the rest of his life.

I recall a Chinese story about a historical figure named Chen Sheng who later launched the first and the largest civil rebellion in Chinese history against the Qin Dynasty in the year 209 B.C. Chen Sheng was a young farmhand hired to till land. During the intense summer heat, he put down his tiller to wipe out his sweat, and said to a fellow farmhand, "If I become rich and noble, I will not forget you." The friend laughed, "How can you be rich and noble, if you are just a farmhand." Chen Sheng sighed deeply: "How can a sparrow understand the aspirations of a swan?" Yes, I will repeat this story to my friends.

So, it is with excitement, anticipation, and also trepidation and ambivalence that we are seeing through Robert's application process for the Academy and that we will trust our son to the Academy if he is accepted.

Away and away, far and high, the swan will fly!

Thoughts and Opinions

1. If you had asked your parents to write a letter about yourself, in your opinion, what would they be writing about you?

2. How would your parents evaluate you as a student?

3. What key words would you be looking for in their letters?

VII

LITERATURE REVIEWS

A | A Never-ending Cycle

Some people see the constant struggle of humanity as a never−ending cycle; a cycle that revolves around the same adversities from the past. Lorraine Hansberry's play, *A Raisin in the Sun* addresses issues that many American families faced during the early 1950s. Hansberry single−handedly reveals the social dilemmas that had never been exposed to the American public. She does so by presenting economical and social hardships of an African−American family, the Youngers. The issues that Hansberry strongly emphasizes in the play are the relationship between husbands and wives and the working class struggle to achieve the American dream. With its ability to connect to audiences of all backgrounds, the play was widely recognized as a factor that changed America's view of its social framework. Due to the existence of these issues today, the present−day audiences can make connections to dilemmas of the past through the play. Therefore, the continuing popularity of *A Raisin in the Sun* shows that the play is as relevant to contemporary audiences as it was when it first appeared.

A man's role and decisions in a household are somewhat dominant over those of women in the 1950s and today's time period. Walter Lee Younger, the main supporter of the Youngers, is a prideful African American who believes he holds greater importance and more power than his wife, Ruth. When Walter's son, Travis, asks Ruth for fifty cents, Ruth hushes him in thought of the family's economic trouble. Upon hearing this, Walter steps into the character of the dominant male of the family: "What you tell the boy things like that for? (Reaching down into his pants with a rather important gesture) Here, son -," (31). Walter acts in defiance against Ruth and her decision to save the fifty cents. More specifically, as the head male of the household, Walter overrules Ruth's opinions and emphasizes his superiority over the women in the house. This type of relationship between husbands and wives still lingers in the contemporary society despite cultural or ethnic differences. Men feel the need to maintain their power, which can be presented as inequality in social status. Including this form of sexism, which is focused significantly in Hansberry's play, many social dilemmas are found relevant to audiences of the past and the present.

Achieving the American Dream was a goal of many Americans in the working class of the 50s. Beneatha Younger, a witty African-American student, dreams of becoming a doctor. However, her dream is deferred due to the lack of economical support from her family. Every morning, Walter bitterly irritates Beneatha about the irrationality of her dream and its costs of achieving it. When Walter senselessly asks Beneatha how she will afford medical school, she replies, "…forgive me for ever wanting to be anything at all! FORGIVE ME, FORGIVE ME, FORGIVE ME!" Beneatha cries in desperation for her dream to be achieved and the economic obstacle to be broken. The struggle of achieving a dream in the low class of society was common in the 1950s. Many average Americans faced a hindrance on their path to success. The level of difficulty to obtain success in the twentieth century is no different than in the 1950s. The contemporary audiences who read and watch this play can relate to this struggle presented nearly half a century ago.

All the issues focused in Hansberry's play directly relate to audiences of the past and the present. These issues undoubtedly transformed the "social fabric and consciousness of the nation" (Introduction). Social dilemmas, such as the inequality of a man's power versus a woman's and an individual's battle against obstacles that are in the way of success, circle our society interminably. As Beneatha claims in the play, changes in society or efforts from successful individuals cannot heal these dilemmas. The cycle will continue, and this concept is significant to the growing popularity of *A Raisin in the Sun.*

B Zora Neale Hurston

The article called "Out of Obscurity" describes the life of Zora Neale Hurston, a remarkable writer with astounding achievements. Hurston portrays a very persistent person, as she lives and accepts poverty, rejection, contentment, and fame. She worked many jobs, such as a waitress or a lady's maid, to reach her lifelong dreams. As a child, she wanted to see the world and experience her native cultures, which she took great interest in her writings. Most of her writing pieces reflected her own life and her passion for colored traditions and folklore. For example, *Jonah's Gourd Vine* displays her parents' marriage and her father's life as a minister. Though she received disapproval of her writing by many educated scholars, Hurston continued to write about the black's struggle with racial treatments.

Zora Neale Hurston was a powerful and influential woman of the 1920s. Her sense of independence is admirable, and she is classified as "pioneering feminist". Hustron learned from the best, such as her classmates in

Howard University, Langston Hughe sand other celebrated intellectuals. Although many her personal life details are in question, one cannot doubt her significant influence in American Literature.

I feel that Zora Neale Hurston had lived an accomplished life, a one which she never lost her dreams and passions in life. She presented the blacks in a way no one could, combining folklore and personal viewpoints of the blacks. It surprised me the most that she lived her life through poverty, when her career as a writer was successful and flourishing. I felt that the last few years of her life consisted of the exact amount of determination as her earlier years of life.

Ⅷ
COMMENTARY

A. The National Debt

B. Freedom for Blacks

C. Teen Pregnancy

D. The People's Princess

E. Driving Age

F. Jazz

A The National Debt

While society progresses into a more technological and money-oriented civilization, people fail to realize the problems that result. Many citizens of the United States have yet to acknowledge the federal debt as a concern, because all they hear from the media is the success of American industries and marketing. However, the economy of the "most powerful" nation is at a downfall, despite the improvements and prosperity of medical advancements and other industries.

As the federal officials continue to practice surplus spending and tax cuts in favor of current citizens' financial situations, the nation is further entangled in disorder. An Oxford University graduate and economist, Tejvan Pettinger claims, "US National debt is currently, $9.7 trillion. It is forecast to rise to, at least, $11.3 trillion, possibly more with financial bail out by the end of 2009. In the coming years, the National debt could become an ever increasing burden fort he US economy." In other words, the nearly $10 trillion debt will gradually increase with time, if no actions are taken to minimize the debt. Although the national debt has yet to significantly harm US citizens, the instability of the economy calls for a swift and decisive action, for the ten trillion dollar deficit will ultimately result in an unfavorable state of inflation, leading to a decrease of foreign investments in the US Treasury and disadvantages to the welfare of citizens in the future.

The more money we borrow, the deeper pitfall the economy of the United States will experience, leading to a more unstable country than that of today. As the need for capital grows accordingly with additional schools, community projects and the increasing population, the higher the debt will increase. The nation will dig a greater debt, forcing the government to borrow more money from other countries. However, the limit of borrowing money from other countries will soon be reached. Therefore, the government will eventually need to depend on domestic ways, in order to fund education, civil projects, and social security.

One of the ways the government will try to collect money is through bonds. Bonds are types of securities sold as "loans" to the government. The federal government sells bonds to holders, citizens or international investors, with the promise to pay back interest in addition to the principle amount. These debt securities are considered more stable than equity securities, such as stock shares. However, bonds are not well protected in times of economic instability, like the present. For instance, say the government decides to print more currency. Since more currency flows into the economic system, each dollar is devalued, thus leading to inflation. Because the government loses the value of each dollar, while the prices of goods remain the same, the government will be coerced to print extra currency, eventually furthering the process of inflation. Thus, at times of inflation, the devaluation of each dollar also devalues the value of bonds; people will sell bonds, leading to higher interest rates on bonds and higher debt interest payments." Higher interest payments make it harder on people to pay back the debt, while the national debt gradually increases. Thus, inflation is fatal to a nation's economy, when the federal debt is too large to solve at once. Furthermore, inflation will greatly damage America's economy with its many dire consequences such as loss of homes and unemployment.

The federal debt will not only harm financial matters at home, but also the international exchanges with foreign investors. The US Treasury consists of investments from citizens as well as foreigners. Foreigners invest in the economy through purchases of bonds and stock shares of US industries and companies. Because American industries generate exceptional productivity in goods, foreigners are attracted to invest in the United States.

Also, due to lower taxes on investments and higher wages than those at home, foreigners fund US markets and industries to gain more wealth. However, as the federal deficit gradually guides the nation into inflation, foreigners will hesitate to invest in an unstable economy. An economics professor at Charwell College states, "If investors see inflation is getting out of control, people will not want to hold bonds. Foreign investors will sell their securities and this will cause devaluation in the currency." Given that foreign securities help maintain the flow of money in the US economy, a decrease in these foreign investments will ultimately drive the economy in to even more debt.

Furthermore, extra printing of currency and deterioration of the economy will result in higher inflation, which sends uninviting messages to prospective investors. With investors busily selling bonds, the demand for US Treasury will continue to decrease. Kimberly Amadeo, the publisher of About.com: US Economy, a part of *The New York Times*, claims that the"…diminished demand for U.S. Treasuries will increase interest rates, thus slowing the economy." An increase in interest rates will result in a decrease in demands for loans and uses of banking systems. More importantly, an increase in interest rates is a future impairment to the nation's economy, for those who already owe money to the government must be able to pay back loans that have multiplied by high interest rates. Thus, increasing disinterest of US Treasuries will significantly worsen the situations for US citizens. Money cycles around national affairs and international businesses; in consequence, a flawed branch of the worldwide capital cycle can create disorder in the global system. More specifically, a downfall in foreign investments in US industries generates setbacks in the nation because resources and funds for merchandise production will reduce in great numbers.

Despite the lack of concerns for the current state of the economy, the debt will surely impact citizens in the future. President Bush has recently cut taxes for citizens, further increasing the national deficit of ten trillion dollars. Satisfaction from tax cuts prevents citizens from realizing that their personal incomes will be cut dramatically as the digits of the debt multiply. This is so because the government will be pressured to raise progressive income tax rates, as the debt begins to increase aggressively due to current tax cuts. Several citizens express their opinions about the debt to CNN as they remark, "…higher taxes in the future means further loans from other countries have been maxed out. ("National Debt Clock…"). A tax break will allow the citizens to receive a larger portion of their incomes, leaving them content yet unaware of its fiscal effects. However, as less money comes into the federal bank, the debt continues to shoot up in response.

Consequently, the US Treasury must enforce a higher tax rate in the coming years to place America's economy back in a more stable condition. The government will also need more money to pay off social security and other federal programs and projects that need funding without increasing the nation deficit. Thus, the government will increase tax rates, in the near future, to collect the money needed. Though, the national debt has yet to affect citizens in significant ways, and until then, America will remain blissfully unaware of the consequences to come. However, as excessive spending continues and the deficit continues to carry on, people of all classes will undoubtedly be harmed. For example, to business owner s…"the heavy tax that is paid is substantial funds that could most prudently be re–invested in the growth of businesses. But instead must be shoveled out simply to service the interest on the Federal debt." This demonstrates the disadvantages business owners have as the debt increases in result of surplus spending and an unbalanced federal budget.

Another significant, yet concealed factor that will play a role in the state of the economy is the age of the country's population. Due to prior baby boomers and the gradual decrease in births, politicians and government officials claim the nation's population as aging. This interpretation demonstrates that there is a higher percentage of men and women than that of children. The aging population can take part in the downfall of the nation's economy. As the population ages, there will be a major increase in the demands for social security and health pensions. With high demand for social security, the Department of the Treasury is currently "using the $2.4 trillion Social Security surplus to offset cash shortfalls. This is money taken from what was called, under Clinton, the Social Security "Lock Box." Thus, in 2013, the Government will owe Social Security about $4 trillion dollars" ("Does the National.."). The more money the government spends now to accommodate to cash shortfalls, the less money the federal bank will have in the future to afford social security, especially for the aging population.

Also consider that paying for pensions and health care to an ageing population will do nothing to facilitate economic growth and higher tax revenues. Health care and social security do little to boost the economy. Furthermore, as the older population reaps the benefits the federal government offer, the rest of the population gain nothing but notices of higher tax revenues to alleviate the federal deficit. Many predict that by 2040, there "will be no more capital left in the US Treasury to provide funding for social security and other retirement benefits." Thus, excess spending in favor of the current population will not bring profit to future generation; the burden of this deficit must be lifted now.

Even at this second, the debt of ten trillion dollars is still increasing. The government wants to satisfy current taxpayers to America through taxbreak sand fair interest rates. However, this will only harm citizens of the coming years. Many people find the debt as a useless number to illustrate the status of the United States' economy and as an unnecessary worry to the American economists. They believe so because the industries and US markets have flourished globally. Also, America is recognized as one of the most powerful and wealthiest nations in the world. However, such large federal deficit can lead to inflation, which will provoke distress in the nation. Furthermore, if inflation cannot be controlled, the nation being afflicted will lose financial interactions with other nations and experience hardships in its economy in the future.

Thus, governments can hopefully establish stable budget plans that limit spending and induce revenue. Also, the officials must realize that even though current citizens may be satisfied with tax cuts, the future generations of America is gradually ruined. The high debt should be a concern regardless of the present or future, however.

B Freedom for Blacks

The word freedom signifies the equality all races should have; however, civil rights activists, along with many black and white citizens of America, believed that African Americans in the US did not have equality. This word is the main concept of the programs set up by civil rights organizations such as Congress of Racial Equality and Student Nonviolent Coordinating Committee, hence the names: Freedom Summer and Freedom Riders. Such projects were conducted to register blacks to vote and eliminate legal segregation in transportation systems in mostly southern states. Many heroic figures of the Civil Rights Movement, such as Martin Luther King Jr. and Rosa Parks, are praised for their impressive effort and endurance through the strenuous fight for equality. White university students significantly advanced the movement as well, but America fails to give the same amount of recognition to their achievements. Through their relentless participation in Freedom Summer and Freedom Rides, white university students effectively promoted black civil rights and extensively raised awareness of racial injustice to the general public, which compelled individuals to reevaluate their moral standards.

Despite the hardships to achieve progress towards racial equality, white university students voluntarily participated in civil rights programs and nonviolently challenged discriminatory laws. Although the Fifteenth Amendment in the Constitution gave blacks the rights to vote in 1870, many African Americans were unable to practice their rights due to hindrances organized by the local governments. These included literacy tests and poll taxes, which the majority of blacks could not pass. Also, segregation in schools, buses, and public facilities still lingered in the southern states. Freedom Summer and Freedom Rides enabled students and other activists to nonviolently protest in southern states such as Mississippi; most hoped to attract the attention of unaware citizens in America through the media. University students, both black and white, from Yale, Stanford, and Cornell etc., created organizations and protests to challenge these legal injustices. Young white activists positively influenced the progression of the civil rights movement, suffering through physical abuse as well as the degradation of their reputation.

By spreading information of black voting rights through Freedom Summer, white university students startled the American public and influenced citizens to reconsider their moral values. In the summer of 1964, volunteers, consisting of black and white university students and other civil rights activists, gathered to launch a project called Freedom Summer. Its main goal was to register African Americans to practice their voting rights. The absurdity of any white individual promoting voting rights of a black man attracted media and helped achieve some secondary goals from the project: "mobilizing volunteer white college students from the North to join them, the coalition scored a major public relations coup as hundreds of reporters came to Mississippi from around the country to cover the voter-registration campaign" (*Congress of Racial*…). White student involvement in Freedom Summer provoked the attention of the general public. As reporters poured in "from around the country", more information about the black voter-registration was heavily televised all throughout the nation. Even though watching these white-skinned youths protest on television did not compel the citizens to become advocates, it educated the uninformed. Meanwhile, when Freedom Summer began, many activists, whether black or white, were under grave danger from white communities. When it was reported that Andrew Goodman and Michael Schwerner, two white civil rights activists, were murdered by severe beating and lethal weapons, "the murders made headlines all over the country, and provoked an outpouring of national support for the Civil Rights Movement" (Simkin). Those who were already aware of anti−black behavior throughout the nation were forced to reevaluate their outlook on the racial injustice. The matter gained a great deal of interest and concern when two white individuals were murdered by their own people. Freedom Summer was a huge success in rousing alarm and anxiety in the American public. However, it was not the only main project to promote black civil rights and build an army the supporters of the movement.

With the nonviolent protests against segregation laws, Freedom Riders provoked a commotion that significantly impacted the progress towards achieving equality within the African American race. Organized by CORE, Congress on Racial Equality, in 1961, Freedom Rides practiced civil disobedience to abolish segregation in public transportation. Freedom Riders, blacks and whites, participated in the nonviolent protests and were physically abused or killed in response. Despite the harsh reaction from the southern white mobs, the Freedom Riders continued. These whites and blacks sat together in buses and ate together in restaurants, and broke segregation laws. Enraged white mobs in Mississippi beat the Freedom Riders with lead and wooden baseball bats, in response to the interaction between both races. In result, "alarmed by the violence, President Kennedy… strike[d] a deal with the state officials from Mississippi to ensure that the Freedom Riders would have safe passage to

Jackson" (Lisker). If the young white advocates had not participated in the Freedom Rides, then no integration would have ensued. President Kennedy was only "alarmed by the violence", which resulted from the integration of the black and white activists. Therefore, the blacks alone could not have reached the attention of the federal government. Furthermore, the Freedom Rides caused a number of companies to desegregate in the fear of future boycotts. Secondly, the participation of white students changed the responses of the general public to these acts of civil disobedience.

The introduction of the book, *Freedom Riders: 1961 and the Struggle for Racial Justice*, states that many Americans felt extreme anxiety when the media revealed young whites being beaten to fight for an issue that was once considered unimportant(Arsenault). By forcing the issue of racial prejudice on mainstream, the white students also forced their peers to reevaluate social values and morals. Thus, as the young generation changed its perspectives of racism in the nation, it caused those of greater age to think about injustices.

In conclusion, many people choose to be indifferent towards social issues in fear of unnecessary disturbance of peace. However, the involvement of white students from the North in the fight forced Americans to reconsider their judgments on blacks and their rights. These university students enabled the issue to reach the attention at a nation–wide level. They also provoked an affection of care or worry in the public. Their participation in the civil rights movement advanced its progress drastically and initiated the start of the protests at a national level. Thus, white university students deserve more recognition and praise than they receive now, for their efforts and sacrifices to let blacks be free.

C Teen Pregnancy

Pleasure is short-lived and fleeting. However, it is the temptation that some teens are lured into, despite the huge risk involved. Teen pregnancy is a critical issue our society encounters, especially in the Santa Clara County. The consequences of pregnancy and its requirement of responsibility and patience are hidden under a shadow of pleasure and attraction. Many teenage mothers attend high schools with their child in hand. Thus, the unfortunate result of this issue greatly influences youth learning environment and the society's atmosphere.

In a recent survey, Santa Clara County recorded a total of 1,366 babies born from teenage girls(ages15-19). The total number is high, even though it has dropped significantly from 1997. Many of these babies are born into hands of mothers, who do not have the experience of supporting another life in addition to their own. It is confirmed that babies born from teenage mothers are less likely to visit medical care. In other words, the foundation to raise a child by teenage mothers is unstable and insecure. Also, the stress and hardships involved with teen birth will provoke overwhelmed and devastated emotions to the young mothers.

The child's life and health must be taken into consideration as well. Babies born to teenage mothers will not receive the full attention and care they require. For example, many children at my school's day care are tended to by volunteers, at a ratio of 6:1, while the mothers are in class. However, more importantly, who desires to be born as a mistake? Even worse, a mistake that sprang from simple, temporary pleasure. As shown, the consequences are unfavorable to the teens and the child.

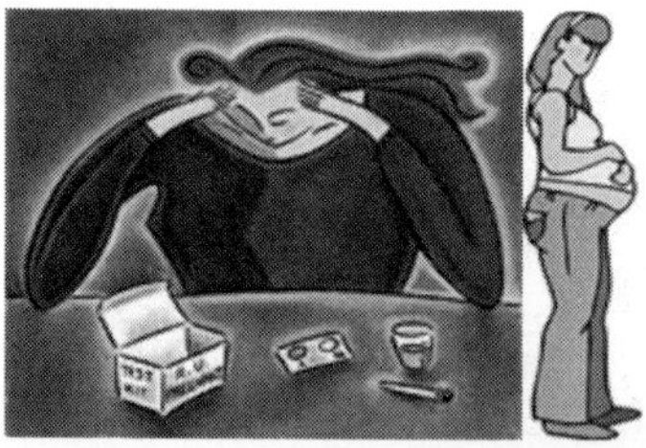

D The People's Princess

"No one who knew Diana will ever forget her. Millions of others who never met her, but felt they knew her, will remember her," said Queen Elizabeth II (Gray). Princess Diana of Wales captured the hearts and eyes of men and women all around the world. However, Diana's greatest achievements were her kindness and active participation in charities. Her impact on the world and her people is to last forever, despite her death on August 31, 1997. She was a person with love and compassion for others, and a person that can delineate the hopes, determination, and heart that an individual has to make a difference.

Princess Diana followed her sympathetic concerns, and was determined to help others; therefore was greatly honored for her effort. Before her marriage to Prince Charles, she was raised by her father in an aristocratic background and became known as Lady Diana Spencer. Diana was known to be not as intelligent as the common princesses, but she had the goodwill and heart of innocence. People expected her beauty and charm to carry her to stardom; however she managed to crack the preconception. With her dedication towards charities for the helpless, self-confidence to be an inspiration to women, and motivation to shed light on the bigotry towards the sick, Princess Diana of Wales demonstrated her kindness and strength as she positively impacted the world.

Princess Diana rescued a nation with her dedication to the helpless from landmines. She volunteered in the International Red Cross and visited landmines in Angola, a southern country in Africa. In addition, she attended classes elaborating upon the dangers the villagers and citizens of Angola are subjected to. As she toured the perilous site, Diana attracted the media with pictures to educate the world of the dangers of the landmines. She spent a great deal of time with landmine survivors, giving each of them a sense of safety in the future. She assured them safety, for she encouraged nation's governments to prohibit use of landmines. More specifically, she was significantly admired for, "…her influence on the governments of the UK and other nations, in their signing of the Ottawa Treaty in December 1997 which created an international ban on the use of anti-personnel landmines"(Charity). Through her influence, Princess Diana managed to protect villages and citizens living near landmines, and to give them comfort in their living conditions. She also sheltered the villagers' security and prevented most future harm from the landmines. Diana possessed tremendous courage to risk her own life by touring dangerous landmines and generosity to contribute effort on a country that she has no obligation towards. With the prohibition from the Ottawa Treaty, Diana saved many lives from physical damage and crucial injuries. As Princess Diana of Wales defined the common portrayal of a hero saving lives from physical danger, she saved many by being her self and staying strong.

As a role model for many women around the world, Princess Diana lived the dreams of many women and became their inspiration. Princess Diana lived a modern day fairy tale: marrying a prince and living the dream life filled with riches and fame. She also had two handsome sons, who were the heirs of United Kingdom, Canada, and Australia. However, not all fairy tales have a happy ending. It became apparent that Diana was not Prince Charles' first love. As frequent arguments and problems surfaced, the royal couple soon divorced. As she had experienced pain of separation from before due to her parent's divorce, she stood alone, but strong. Along with her associations to 110 humanitarian organizations, charm, and beauty, Diana withheld many interests from men. However, it is said, "…but her hold on women was stronger still. Grown women, no matter bruised by reality, remember those romantic dreams. Diana lived them…an inspiration to every woman anywhere who faced the trauma and challenge of sudden independence" (Gray). She led women and supported those who had to face this independence from family by showing them strength and faith in herself. Princess Diana continued her journey towards world renown with associations of charity and goodwill. She represented women's inner strength and keenness, which directly increased confidence of women who watched and adored her. Furthermore, it was a traumatizing time for her; she was soon diagnosed with postpartum depression and health malfunction. However, she inspired all women around the world to have faith and hope, just as she did with her life and goals. Along with her beliefs in giving strength to those who suffer the same as she does, she helped change the way the society viewed certain sickness in the world.

Princess Diana had motivation to shed light on the bigotry of the sick as she began to interact with those less fortunate than she. Diana's best know achievement was depicted in a photograph with an AIDS patient. This picture changed views of many around the world that had the impressions that AIDS patients must be separated from society. She also used the media to acknowledge such epidemics, along with speeches to teach about depression. Another, she raised awareness of poverty and other heavy disturbances such as discrimination. In an interview aired on ABC on November 1995, Diana conveys, "Then I found myself being more and more involved with people who were rejected by society – with, I'd say, drug addicts, alcoholism, battered this, battered that – and I found an affinity there" *(Princess Diana Speaks). The idea of her interacting with those rejected by society alleviates the world's hostility against the ill. In further detail, Princess Diana engages with her oppositions in society and brings different social levels closer. Thus, it is an idea that she was attracted to the idea of union among social classes and healed the pain those discriminated received. Princess Diana also made friends with gay people and Muslims, which eased the tension within the society of discrimination.

Overall, "she showed the world that people with AIDS deserved not isolation, but compassion. It helped change world opinion, helped give hope to people with AIDS, and helped save lives of people at risk. She was 'the people's princess'; she had gay and black friends; she spoke of her postpartum depression" (Elliot). Princess altered the hatred in the world as she demonstrated the preconceived portrayals of certain groups were false. With so much media attention she brought upon the discriminated, she brought the world closer together. She used her fame and fortune to show the world that the sick needed support and compassion instead of the bigotry they receive.

With her considerable fame and wealth, Princess Diana supported the less fortunate to the best of her abilities.

She was involved in 110 charity organizations with profound dedication and corrected the negative preconception of the sickness all around the world. "She translated her own pain not into bitterness and withdrawal but into a genuine desire to comfort the suffering of others" (Gray). She was a great contributor to the cliché that one person can definitely make a difference. Diana affected the world greatly with her good heart, goodwill, and compassion for others. More importantly, Princess Diana brought the world as one; she gathered the royalties with the poor, the sick with the healthy, and the brokenhearted with the loved. Therefore, anyone can impact the world, if one has the hope in his or herself and the dedication to contribute comfort to those unfortunate, as Diana did. Hence, she was recognized as the world's role model, the world's princess.

<Reflective Abstract>

As I was writing this essay, I began to realize the actual meaning of 'power of one'. Princess Diana was a great woman to honor and admire, and her stories explained to me the power with her determination and hopes. I realized that one person can really make a difference if he or she has the compassion to start a change. Even though comprehending and connecting Diana's accomplishments to the theory of "power of one" was challenging, I still felt afterwards that I understood why she was so greatly honored for her work and beauty. It definitely was amazing to know that a woman can have so much inner-strength, another reason to greatly respect and appreciate her work.

First, researching for Princess Diana was difficult, for most information was similar and had the same background details. Therefore, finding three components with which she benefited the world consumed great amount of time and thought. Also, as the paper deadline came closer, I had trouble organizing my paper and connecting each idea with the thesis. However, the research notes came in handy, for I had most of my evidences and its analysis written out in bullet point format beforehand. With the process of the research notes, I understood and discovered more in depth about Princess Diana, making the paper easier to write. Next, because Princess Diana was an inspiring and strong woman, I felt passionate about the concept of the paper. Furthermore, I efficiently researched for Princess Diana's charity work for I was anxious to see how she benefited the world.

Overall, I feel good about what I learned throughout the researching process. Even though I felt that my writing techniques were weak, the new insights I gained was a much more proficient experience.

E Driving Age

As vehicles become more common and easier to utilize, they have occupied every inch of space in communities. Such drastic evolution has resulted in more accidents and deaths per year, especially in teens, inflaming protests about legal driving age. So should the legal age be raised to 18? This highly controversial matter has been an issue for more than a decade, with respectable arguments for both sides.

"Inexperience and immaturity are the two things that work against teens. Those are the primary reasons teens have high crash rates compared with drivers who are just a little bit older." said Russell J. Rader, spokesman for the Insurance Institute for Highway Safety. The childish and rebellious reputation of youths today has worried parents and adults nationwide of teenage driving. I am currently a senior in high school at the age of 17. However, I have yet to attain a driver's license due to parents' protest against it. They have claimed that I am not prepared to drive, a sign of independence and adulthood. Furthermore, many adults believe that age directly influences driving, for youths do not have enough experience to judge right and wrong. In other words, teens tend to break driving laws, including drunk driving and speeding.

Although there is some truth to the relation between immaturity and driving, it does not apply to all circumstances. According to a nationwide study by the Insurance Institute for Highway Safety, the number of fatal accidents involving 16-year-old drivers dropped by 26 percent between 1993 and 2003. Also, this statistic was calculated while the number of 16 year-old drivers increased by about 20 percent. Therefore, it is safe to claim that due to only few high-profile crashes, minors are penalized for dangerous driving. Also, no one knows how exactly raising the legal age will ease the high accident and death rates. I have numerous friends who drive, even since the age of 16, and have yet to be in an accident. They consider driving as a privilege, a chance to be independent from their parents, who work and find no time to drive their kids.

Perhaps the fairest way to settle this matter is to not raise the legal age but to intensify driver's education and punishments. Whatever way the issue will settle, the accident rates on the road will remain high, not due to teenage driving, but irresponsible driving.

Statistics found: "Questions complicate driving-age debate" by The Republican

F Jazz

Jazz is a very influential type of music of American culture, and has been around for almost 100 years. It was originated from New Orleans, when brass bands, made of black men, played during the War of 1812. Jazz evolved from many different aspects, including the blues and spirituals. Jazz bands in the past consisted of instruments such as the trumpets, trombones, clarinets, saxophones, and the drums. Entertainment was not the sole motivation of the music, however, it was considered as "basic human expression".

It is known to many that jazz gained its popularity during the Roaring Twenties. The Harlem Renaissance introduced the music to the American society as clubs and other social events became popular. People of all ages and gender were drawn to the catchy and creative music styles of jazz. According to the article, "Music!...To Characterize The Age" the rhythms of jazz were simplified versions of complex rhythms of African music. Soloists of jazz improvised their own flavor in the music. For example, many soloists "shifted accents to weak beats and emphasized syncopation." One of the most famous jazz entertainers was Louis "Satchmo" Armstrong. He was considered one of the best entertainers with his unique improvised solo performances. A genius of music, Armstrong added scat singing to his performances to draw in large audiences. He was also one of the first to discover swing, which gained its period of fame.

As Americans became more passionate for jazz, new styles of the music emerged. In the 1940s, after the WWII, a style called Bop was invented. It competed with swing, which was another style to emerge from jazz. The techniques of swing primarily concerned with dancing, while Bop inspired listening. Many considered Bebop as a form of art, for the style was sophisticated and expressive. This may have been the start of music of sensitivity and emotion, rather than catchy, entertaining music of dance.

In conclusion, jazz awakened from American culture as an expression of creativity and emotions. Today, jazz is still influential in American lives, for many music styles, such as swing and bebop, emerged throughout several decades. It is safe to state that jazz was one of the few miracles that attracted interests of all races. Its unique rhythms and spontaneity gave rise to many musical prodigies and other types of musical expressions.

IX
OTHER ADAPTED STORIES

A The Story of an Hour

(The story originally written by Kate Chopin adapted by C. G. Draper)

They knew that Louise Mallard had a weak heart. So they broke the bad news softly, Her husband, Brently, was dead.

"There was a train accident, Louise," said her sister Josephine, quietly.

Her husband's friend, Richards, stood with Josephine. Richards brought the news, but Josephine told the story. She spoke in broken sentences.

"Richards .... was at the newspaper office. News of the accident came. Louise . . Louise, Brently's name was on the list. Brently . . was killed, Louise."

Louise did not hear the story coldly, like some women would. She could not close her mind or her heart to the news. Like a sudden storm, her tears broke out. She cried loudly in her sister's arms. Then, just as suddenly, the tears stopped. She went to her room alone. She wanted no one with her.

In front of the window stood an empty chair. She sat

down and looked out the window. She was very tired after her tears. Her body felt cold, her mind and heart were empty.

Outside her window she could see the trees. The air smelled like spring rain. She could hear someone singing far away. Birds sang near the house. Blue sky showed between the clouds. She rested.

She sat quietly, but a few weak tears still fell. She had a young, strong face. But now her eyes showed nothing. She looked out the window at the blue sky. She was not thinking, or seeing. She was waiting.

There was something coming to her. She was waiting for it with fear. What was it? She did not know: she could not give it a name. But she felt it coming out from the sky. It reached her through the sound, the smell, the color of the air,

Slowly she became excited. Her breath came fast, her heart beat faster. She began to see this thing. It wanted to find her and take her. She tried to fight against it. But she could not Her mind was as weak as her two small white hands. Then she stopped fighting against it. A little word broke from her lips.

"free," she said. "Free, free, free!" The emptiness and fear left her. Her eyes showed her excitement. Her heart beat fast, and the blood warmed her body. A sudden feeling of joy excited her.

She did not stop to ask if her joy was wrong. She saw

her freedom clearly. She could not stop to think of smaller things.

She knew the tears would come again when she saw her husband's body, The kind hands, now dead and still. The loving face, now still and gray, But she looked into the future. She saw many long years to come that would belong to her alone. And now she opened her arms wide to those years in welcome.

There would be no one else to live for during those years. She would live for herself alone. There would be no strong mind above hers. Men and women always believe they can tell others what to do and how to think. Suddenly Louise understood that this was wrong. She could breakaway and be free of it.

And yet, she loved him—sometimes. Often she did not.

What did love mean now? Now she understood that freedom is stronger than love.

"Free! Body and mind free! " she said again.

Her sister Josephine was waiting outside the door.

"Please open the door," Josephine cried. "You will make yourself sick. What are you doing in there, Louise? Please, please, let me in! "

"Go away. 1 am not sick." No, she was drinking in life through that open window.

She thought joyfully of all those days before her. Spring days, summer days. All kinds of days that would be her own. She began to hope life would be long. And just yesterday, life seemed so long.

After a while she got up and opened .the door, Her eyes were bright, her cheeks were red. She didn't know how strong and well she looked—so full of joy. They went downstairs, where Richards was waiting.

A man was opening the door. It was Brently Mallard. He was dirty, and tired. He carried a suitcase and an umbrella. He was not killed in the train accident. He didn't even know there was an accident He was surprised at Josephine's sudden cry. He didn't understand why]Richards moved suddenly between them, to hide Louise from her husband.

But Richards was too late.

When the doctors came, they said it was her weak heart They said she died of joy — joy that kills.

Interpretation and Discussion

1. Based on *The Story of an Hour*, by Kate Chopin, what is the main theme of the story?

2. Describe the emotional/mental changes Louis was going through from the beginning to the end.

3. According to the passage, "They said she died of joy." Did she? If not, why not?

4. How does the life of Louis different from your life as a woman?

B The Gift of the Magi

(The story originally written by O. Henry adapted by C. G. Draper)

Della counted her money three times. She had only one dollar and eighty-seven cents. That was all. And tomorrow would be Christmas. What Christmas gift could she buy with only one dollar and eighty-seven cents. Della lay down on the old bed and cried and cried.

Let's leave Della alone for a while and look at her home. The chairs and tables were old and poor, Outside there was a mailbox without mail, and a door without a doorbell. The name on the door said MR. JAMES DILLINGHAM YOUNG.-Della's dear husband Jim.

Delta knew that Jim would be home soon. She dried her eyes and stood up. She looked in the mirror. She began to comb her hair for Jimn. She felt very sad. She wanted to buy Jim a Christmas gift-something good. But what could she do with one dollar and eighty-seven cents? She combed her hair in the mirror and thought Suddenly she had an ides.

Now, Jim and Delta had only two treasures. One was

Jim's gold watch. The other was Della's hair, It was long and brown, and fell down her back. Delta looked in the mirror a little longer, Her eyes were sad, but then she smiled. She put on her old brown coat and her hat She ran out of the house and down the street. She stopped in front of a door which said, MME. SOPHRONIE. HAIR FOR ALL KINDS. Madame Sophronie was fat and seemed too white. The store was dark.

"Will you buy my hair?" Della asked.

"I buy hair," said Madame. "Take off your hat. Let's see your hair." Della took off her hat. Her hair fell down like water, Mme. Sophronie lifted Delta's hair with a heavy hand.

"Twenty dollars," she said. "Give me the money now" said Delta.

Ah! the next two hours flew past like summer wind. Della shopped in many stores for the right gift for Jim. Then she found it—a chain for his gold watch. It was a good chain, strong and expensive. Delta knew the chain would make Jim happy. Jim had a cheap chain for his watch, but this chain was much better. It would look good with the gold watch. The chain cost twenty—one dollars. Della paid for the chain, and ran home with eighty—seven cents.

At seven o'clock Delta made coffee and started to cook dinner. It was almost dinner time. Jim would be home soon. He was never late. Della heard Jim outside. She looked in the mirror again. "Oh! I hope Jim doesn't kill me! " Della smiled, but her eyes were wet. "But what could Ido with only one dollar and eighty-seven cents?"

The door opened, and Jim came in and shut it. His face was thin and quiet. His coat was old, and he had no hat. He was only twenty-two. Jim stood still and looked at Delta. He didn't speak. His eyes were strange. Delta suddenly felt afraid. She did not understand him. She began to talk very fast. "Oh, Jim, dear, why do you look so strange? Don't look at me like that. 1 cut my hair and sold it. 1 wanted to buy you a Christmas gift. It will grow again-don't be angry. My hair grows very fast, Say 'Merry Christmas, 'dear, and let's be happy. You don't know what I've got for you-it's beautiful."

"You cut your hair?" Jim spoke slowly.

"I cut it and sold it," Della answered. "Don't you like me now? I'm still me, aren't 1?"

"You say that your hair is gone?"Jim asked again.

"Don't look for it, it's gone," Della said. "Be good to me, because it's Christmas. Shall we have dinner now, Jim?"

Jim seemed to wake up. He smiled. He took Della in his arms.

Let us leave them together for a while. They are happy, rich or poor. Do you know about the Magi? The Magi were wise men who brought Christmas gifts to the baby Jesus. Perhaps Jim and Della do not seem wise. They lost the two great treasures of their house. But I want to tell you that they were wise. People like Jim and Della are always wiser than others. Everywhere they are wiser. They are the magi.

Interpretation and Discussion

1. Why was magi at the end written in small letters?

2. Respond to the last sentence: "They are the magi." Do you agree with the author?

3. In your opinion, define what love is.

C Love of Life

(The story originally written by Jack London adapted by C. G. Draper)

Two men walked slowly through the low water of a river. They were alone in the cold, empty land. All they could see were stones and earth. It was fall, and the river ran cold over their feet. They carried blankets on their backs. They had guns, but no bullets; matches, but no food.

"I wish we had just two of those bullets we hid in the camp," said the first of the men. His voice was tired. The other man did not answer.

Suddenly the first man fell over a stone. He hurt his foot badly, and he cried out. He lay still for a moment, and then called: "Hey, Bill, I've hurt my foot." Bill didn't stop or look back. He walked out of the river and over the hill. The other man watched him. His eyes seemed like the eyes of a sick animal. He stood up. "Bill" he cried again. But there was no answer, Bill kept walking.

"Bill!"

The man was alone in the empty land. His hands were

cold, and he dropped his gun. He fought with his fear, and took his gun out of the water. He followed slowly after Bill. He tried to walk lightly on his bad foot. He was alone, but he was not lost. He knew the way to their camp. There he would find food, bullets, and blanket. He must find them soon. Bill would wait for him there. Together they would go south to the Hudson Bay Company. They would find food there, and a warm fire. Home. The man had to believe that Bill would wait for him at the camp. If not, he would die. He thought about the food in the camp. And the food at the Hudson Bay Company. And the food he ate two days ago. He thought about food and he walked. After a while the man found some small berries to eat. The berries had no taste, and did not fill him. But he knew he must eat them.

In the evening he hit his foot on a stone and fell down. He could not get up again. He lay still for a long time. Later, he felt a little better and got up. He made a fire. He could cook only hot water, but he felt warmer. He dried his shoes by the fire. They had many holes. His feet had blood on them. His foot hurt badly. He put his foot in a piece of his blanket. Then he slept like a dead man. He woke up because he heard an animal near him. He thought of meat and took his gun. But he had no bullets. The animal ran away, The man stood up and cried out. His foot was much worse this morning. He took out a small bag that was in his blanket. It was heavy—fifteen pounds. He didn't know if he could carry it. But he couldn't leave it behind. He had to take it with him. He had to be strong enough. He put it into his blanket again.

That day his hunger grew worse, worse than the hurtin his foot. Many times he wanted to lie down, but hunger made him go on. He saw a few birds. Once he tried to catch one, but it flew away. He felt tired and sick. He forgot to follow the way to the camp. In the afternoon he found some green plants. He ate them fast, like a horse. He saw a small fish in a river, He tried to catch it with his cup. But the fish swam away into a hole. The man cried like a baby, first quietly, then loudly. He cried atone in that empty world.

That night he made a fire again, and drank hot water. His blanket was wet, and his foot hurt. He could think only of his hunger, He woke up cold and sick. The earth and sky were gray. He got up and walked, he didn't know where. But the small bag was with him. The sun came out again, and he saw that he was lost. Was he too far north? He turned toward the east. His hunger was not so great, but he knew he was sick. He stopped often. He heard wolves, and knew that deer were near him. He believed he had one more bullet in his gun. It was still empty. The small bag became too heavy, The man opened the bag. It was full of small pieces of gold. He put half the gold in a piece of his blanket and left it on a rock. But he kept his gun. There were bullets in that camp.

Days passed, days of rain and cold. One day he came to the bones of a deer. There was no meat on the bones. The man knew wolves must be near. He broke the bones and ate like an animal. Would he, too, be only bones tomorrow? And why not? This was life, he thought. Only life hurt. There was no hurt in death. To die was to sleep. Then why was he not ready to die? He could not see or feel. The hunger, too, was gone. But he walked and walked.

One morning he woke up beside a river. Sun light was warm on his face. A sunny day, he thought. Perhaps he could find his way to the camp. His eyes followed the river. He could see far. The river emptied into the sea. He saw a ship on that silver sea. He shut his eyes. He knew there could be no ship, no seas, in this land. He heard a noise behind him, and turned back. A wolf, old and sick, was following him. 1 know this is real, he thought. He turned again, but the sea and the ship were still there. He didn't understand it. He tried to remember. What did the men at the Hudson Bay Company say about this land? Was he walking north, away from the camp, toward the sea? The man moved slowly toward the ship. He knew the sick wolf was following him. In the afternoon, he found more bones left by wolves. The bones of a man! Beside the bones was a small bag of gold, like his own. Ha! Bill carried his gold to the end, he thought. He would take Bill's gold to the ship. He would have the last laugh on Bill. His laughing sounded like the low cry of an animal. The wolf cried back to the man, and the man stopped laughing. How could he laugh about Bill's bones? He could not take Bill's gold. He left the gold near the bones.

The man was very sick, now. He walked more and more slowly. His blanket was gone. He lost his gold, then his gun, then his knife. Only the wolf stayed with him hour after hour. At last the man could go no further. He fell down. The wolf came close to him. It weakly bit his hand. The man hit the wolf and it went away, But it did not go far. It waited. The man waited. After many hours the wolf came back again. It was going to kill the man. But the man was ready, He held the wolfs mouth closed, and he got on top of the sick wolf. He held the animal still. Then he bit it with his last strength. He tasted the wolfs blood in his mouth. Only love of life gave him enough strength. He held the wolf with his teeth and killed it. Later he fell on his back and slept.

The men on the ship saw a strange thing on the land. It did not walk. It was tying on the ground, and it moved slowly toward them—perhaps twenty feet an hour. The men went close to look at it. They could not believe it was a man. Three weeks later the man felt better. He could tell them his story. But there was one strange thing. He could not believe there was enough food on the ship. The men told him there was a lot of food. But he only looked at them with fear. And slowly he began to grow fat. The men thought this was strange. They gave him less food, but still he grew larger and larger—each day he was fatter. Then one day they saw him put a lot of bread under his shirt. They looked in his bed, too, and saw bread under his blanket. The men understood, and left him alone.

Interpretation and Discussion

1. Based on *Love of Life*, how does the title related to the story itself? How does the man show that he loves his life?

2. Who is Bill? Why do you think he didn't stop or look back?

3. Was the man safe on the ship? Did he have enough food to eat? Why was he still afraid?

4. What lesson does the author, Jack London, try to address throughout the story?